I AM <u>SO</u>
THE BOSS OF
YOU

ALSO BY KATHY BUCKWORTH

The Secret Life
of Supermom

Supermom:
A Celebration of All You Do

Journey to the Darkside:
Supermom Goes Home

The BlackBerry Diaries:
Adventures in Modern Motherhood

Shut Up and Eat!:
Tales of Chicken, Children, and Chardonnay

I AM SO THE BOSS OF YOU

An 8-Step Guide to Giving Your Family the "Business"

Kathy Buckworth

McClelland & Stewart

Library and Archives Canada Cataloguing in Publication

Buckworth, Kathy
    I am so the boss of you : an 8-step guide to giving your
family the "business" / Kathy Buckworth.

ISBN 978-0-7710-1748-3

    1. Parenting – Humor. I. Title.

PN6231.P2B83 2013   649'.10207   C2012-906728-8

Published simultaneously in the United States of America by
McClelland & Stewart, a division of Random House of Canada Limited
P.O. Box 1030, Plattsburgh, New York 12901

Library of Congress Control Number: 2012941347

Typeset in Electra by M&S, Toronto
Printed and bound in the United States of America

McClelland & Stewart,
a division of Random House of Canada Limited
One Toronto Street
Suite 300
Toronto, Ontario
M5C 2V6
www.mcclelland.com

1   2   3   4   5   17   16   15   14   13

"Don't look at me in that tone of voice."
– Dorothy Parker

CONTENTS

INTRODUCTION

"You are *not* the boss of me!"

Hey, Mom! Yes, you! The one running to the fridge to pour your eight-year-old son a glass of chocolate milk before he has an epic meltdown (just as you're about to go out with your friends for the first time in six months). How many times have you heard that expression? Come on, you know you have. What's that? You've lost count? Of course.

I don't care whether you're a working mom, a stay-at-home mom, a work-from-home mom, a single mom, or an empty-nest mom. It doesn't matter if you live in North America, Europe, India, or on Planet Xenon. And it makes no difference whether your children are toddling, walking, or driving. If you have children – any children at all – you have heard that annoying pronouncement several thousand times: "You are not the boss of me!" It's been screamed at you by Michael, in the midst of his full-on tantrum in aisle three. It's been spat out by Jennifer, followed by a delightful teenage *stomp-stomp-stomp-slam*. And it's quite possible (you're not entirely sure because you were sleep-deprived at the time) that little Maria strung those seven words together to construct her very first sentence, at the ripe old age of nine months. Just before she threw turnips in your face.

Oh, yes. You've heard that expression. We all have. In fact, we've heard it so many times, and for so many years, that we don't really even hear it anymore. We tune it out. Or maybe we're too busy trying to figure out the "right" way to "parent" our children to pay attention. We've got our noses buried in the latest parenting book, trying to decide what kind of mom we should be: A tiger mom who pushes and prods toward excellence (or at least superiority to other children)? A democratic mom who's willing to vote on the location of the next family holiday and who doesn't ever think about using the Talking Stick in a punitive way? A Helicopter Mom who's there for everything, all the time (even the first day of work)? With so many choices and styles before us (and so many other moms waiting to offer, or publicly blog, judgment on our efforts), it's not hard to see why we've been overlooking the obvious. After twenty or so years of parenting, even I was starting to distrust my own excellent instincts (four kids – all still alive, FYI). And then, in the middle of a two-hour meeting on how to use time more efficiently, it struck me: Why are we working so hard to find the perfect way to parent when we already have an excellent model right in front of us? One that operates efficiently, effectively, and economically? One that millions of people the world over are already employing (though not quite in the way I

mean)? One that goes through an audit process, for good-
ness sake? One that our dear children have been dropping hints about for years?

It's right there – from the mouths of babes, as they say:
"You are *not* the boss of me!"

Oh yes, my little friend, I am! I am the boss of you, in
every imaginable way. Physically, mentally, financially,
parents rule – basically, we're at the top of the food chain.
We get to tell our children when to go to bed, and we get to
choose their mealtimes and what is served at those meals.
We select their extracurricular activities, and, for a (ridiculously) short stretch of time, we even get to pick what they
wear. Perhaps this generation of parents needs to take a
moment to remind itself that we really are The Boss, *El
Presidente*, *Le Grand Fromage*.

So, you're saying, *what's the strategy here? I know I'm
the boss, but it doesn't get me anywhere. I still have no
sleep, no control, and no clean surfaces in my house. And
I still own all the household responsibilities.* There's a difference, you see, between *knowing* that you're the boss
and truly *acting* like you're the boss. Think about it: What
happens when Junior doesn't set the table before dinner?
Or when Little Miss Thing forgets that it's her day to
unload the dishwasher? Or when Skippy over there forgets
to launder his only white shirt for the school concert? You
do it, don't you? Come on, admit it. You know you do. But
what if we were talking about the boardroom and not the
kitchen? What if an employee didn't hand in a report or

failed to complete a project on time? Would you do it for them? Doubtful. Would you put a note in their personal file? Likely!

When I made the transition from working mom to stay-at-home mom, I found myself confused by the sudden lack of control, structure, and, well, subservience – those things I had so enjoyed in the office, leading a team of surly yet somewhat respectful twenty-something employees. I was a director of marketing at a large bank, responsible for the bottom line of several high-profile credit card products. How was it that I could lead a team to greatness (or at least to achieving its quarterly profit objective) yet not be able to convince my two-year-old that he needed to let me tie his shoes before we left the house? Did the fact that I gave some of them a performance review while I allowed others to run wild with no real consequences have anything to do with this disparity? A crazy, insane, possibly brilliant idea began to take hold in my addled brain. What if I were to insert some well-established management-training techniques into the loosey-goosey world of hands-on parenting and home management? What if I were to act like . . . the boss? Of them?

I will admit that my children both balked (the teenagers) and blinked (the younger ones) at the mention of "goal setting" and "performance reviews," but throughout the nine years that I have been on the front lines at home with the children, I've snuck in a few rules and regulations that would make "Neutron" Jack Welch of General Electric

fame proud.[1] (Sadly, unlike Jack, I'm not allowed to fire
10 percent of my employees every year. Not that I haven't
tried to encourage the kids to attend military school in
another province.) Along the way I've realized that there are
huge parallels between running a household and running
a business. From accounting to public relations, human
resources to quality control, the corporate structure can be
easily applied to life with kids. Oh boy! I feel a bunch of
spreadsheets coming on.

Let me explain. It's extremely difficult to have control at
home if you are governing with a child-centric plan that
gives your offspring everything they want and allows them
to have an equal voice in the running of the household.
Even though we should all value the input and opinion of
a junior employee, said employee is not in a position to
make final decisions or, more importantly, to have account-
ability for those decisions. A two-year-old should not be dic-
tating her own bedtime any more than a marketing intern
should be determining the "brand voice" of a successful
and established product.

So why are some of us so willing to hand over the reins
of power to an infant? A toddler? A preschooler, public
schooler, tween, or teen? There's so much that is wrong,

---

[1] Jack Welch was chair and CEO of General Electric (1981–2001). While he ran GE, the company's value rose 4,000 percent. His net worth was at one time estimated to be $720 million.
"Neutron Jack" was known for pulling out bad employees and rewarding his good employees
amply. I could do that. Reward the good kids – the ones who listen to me or kiss up.

or at best inappropriate, about their judgment at each of these ages, and so much that is right about *yours*, that this kind of power transfer just doesn't make any logical or business sense. And yet child-centric parenting models are all the rage, putting forth an idea that the child is equal to the parent. That's the ideal? Are you kidding me?

Be the boss. *Embrace* being the boss. And try – really, really hard – to tune out all of the people who tell you that children are little adults and that their voices need to be heard. We hear them enough, trust me. Sometimes we even *amplify* their voices – via a baby-monitoring speaker system. Hearing is fine. Listening is great. But acting on bad advice is never an appropriate thing to do, corporately or at home.

Still, that's just what many of us are doing these days. When I returned to work following my third maternity leave, I found myself back in a tense corporate environment, managing a diverse team of people. About a week in, I collapsed into my ergonomically correct chair following a session in which a junior employee complained about his work, his hours, his cubicle, hell, even the coffee. I said out loud, "I've just traded supervising one set of whining babies for another." Luckily, as I was at work and not at home, I was able to respond by giving him a bad performance rating (cue light bulb going on). This was in 1999. Almost fifteen years later, a whole new generation of employees in their twenties is still whining and whinging, and the situation is about to get a whole lot worse. Why? Because these young men and women are the products of the original Democratic and Helicopter

Parents. They can do no wrong. They get trophies and medals for simply "showing up," and they control their "superiors" from the moment they are conceived. Or even before. How many parents do you know who let their children decide where they vacation, what they eat, when they sleep?[2]

I recently met with an executive at a public relations firm who said one of her staff wanted a task removed from her job description because it "took too long to do, and it was boring." Really? First of all, shut up. Second, who raised this person? Oh wait, *we* did. We created this monster, and others like her, by making our children believe that they don't have to do anything they really don't want to do. Awesome. And now they're out in the workforce, and they've traded in their overprotective mommies for frustrated supervisors.[3]

I know. It's depressing, right? But it's not too late. There are lots of learning opportunities that parents can and should take advantage of. Many moms will say they are the CEO of their homes but then do nothing to back up this claim. They are, in fact, not good CEOs. But with a little practice, and the right guidance, they could be.

So think of this as a management textbook for your family. You may think that deploying a corporate structure on your children is a bit too rigid and demanding. But the

....

[2] This sets a bad precedent for the little dictators when it comes to life in the real world. Unless they become bankers.
[3] FYI, I told the manager to tell her "I am so the boss of you. Just do it."

paradox is that, just like at work, structure and rules give people the ability to do their own work, take on their own responsibilities, and, ultimately, achieve success. A bad boss micromanages, which is exactly what a lot of parents do today. Don't be that boss. Be a good boss. Follow along to find out how.

EMBRACE THE PHILOSOPHY

Letting Autocratic Parenting Work for You

Are you still with me? Phew. In this age of Democratic Parenting, it's entirely possible that a whole chunk of readers skimmed the introduction and ran screaming into the woods (after asking their children if it was okay to do so), too baffled by the idea of acting like the boss at home to keep turning pages. If you're still here, you're at least willing to entertain the prospect. Congratulations. You're off to a good start. Let's all say it together, shall we? "I am the boss. I am the boss. I am the boss." Excellent! Just make sure you don't say it out loud around the children. Yet.

Because what does being the boss at home really mean? How can we translate this approach into a parenting philosophy that we can all embrace and really use to make our lives simpler and better organized, to give us more control? It's instructive to contrast the idea of Democratic Parenting with what I like to call, with some authority I might add, Autocratic Parenting. Please note: This is not a dictatorship but an autocracy. The kids still have some rights. Like the right to clean their rooms without being asked, for instance.

Think what I'm suggesting is too radical and not at all politically correct? It may be both, but it sure can work. Allow me to illustrate where this book might take you from, and to.

DEMOCRATIC VERSUS AUTOCRATIC PARENTING: A PRIMER

When my son Alex was five years old, he took part in a skating show. In the same show was a friend of his, a little guy with a knack for running his parents around in circles. Minutes before the kids were supposed to take their Teletubby-outfitted selves onto the ice to perform, this mom asked, ever so politely: "Jimmy, would you like to put on your mittens now?"[4] Of course Jimmy said, "No." To which Mom replied, "Well, you have to because the show is about to start." His reply? Wait for it . . . : "No."

You can imagine how this ended. She got angry, and he started crying. She said, "If you don't stop crying and put these mittens on, we're not going to McDonald's afterwards." He kept crying, didn't put the mittens on, and missed the show. And what did his mom and dad do? They took him to McDonald's.

This is Democratic Parenting at its very worst – a situation in which a child is given an inappropriate amount of

....

[4] Name changed to protect the annoying.

power. Why on earth did this mother ask her son to do something he had no choice but to do? It's not like she was about to accept anything but yes. Jimmy was *clearly* the boss of her, and the result, while not catastrophic (how much harm can a Happy Meal do, anyway?), was still a strong indication of how he would rule himself as a child and, more frighteningly, as a teen and as an adult.

Now let's look at the same scenario as it might have been handled by an Autocratic Parent (a.k.a. a boss).

Mom: Jimmy, put your mittens on. Now.
Jimmy: I don't want to.
Mom: Put them on.
Jimmy: Why?
Mom: Because I said so.
Jimmy: But I don't want to.
Mom: That would be entirely relevant had I asked if you *wanted* to. I don't want to make dinner either, but if you don't put those mittens on right now, I will do it for you, and then neither of us will be happy.
Jimmy: They're on!

The Autocratic Parent clearly has the upper hand. Why? My theory is based entirely on anecdotal evidence, but I believe it's because the expectations were clearly laid out and the boundaries were established and adhered to. There was no compromise in a situation that didn't call for compromise. Mittens were needed. Enough said.

Could it be, then, that the Democratic Parenting ideal isn't all it's cracked up to be? Before rushing to judgment, I decided to search for a clear, concise definition to wrap my head around. I came up empty. It seems as if proponents of this child-rearing method are finding it difficult to entirely agree on the basic tenets (never a good sign). So, left to my own devices, I decided to break the phrase down into its two parts to see if it makes any sense. From the *Oxford Dictionary* (the not-so-subtle boldface emphasis is mine):

> **democratic** (adj): relating to or supporting democracy or its principles: democratic countries, democratic government; **favoring** or characterized by social equality; egalitarian: *cycling is a very democratic activity that can be enjoyed by anyone.*
> **parenting:** from the source word *parent* (n): a person's father or mother; a forefather or ancestor; an animal or plant from which new ones are derived; **a source or origin of a smaller or less important part**; an organization or company which owns or controls a number of subsidiaries. (verb): be or act as a mother or father to (someone).

Is it just me or is there a total disconnect here? Maybe even an oxymoronic taint to the phrase? On the one hand you've got "social equality." On the other you've got "a source or origin of a smaller or less important part." Sounds like an oxymoron to me! Pay attention now: Democratic Parenting *should* be an oxymoron in your house. If it's not, you're in trouble. If the Teletubby scene above wasn't enough to convince you, here are a few more examples of how the two parenting styles actually play out (see page 14).

As you can see, one of the great benefits of Autocratic Parenting is a greatly diminished amount of "talking time." Parenting can be a huge time suck, even more so when you allow young children to have an equal say or "voice" in every decision you make.

But that's not the only way Democratic Parenting causes extra and unnecessary work. It can also lead to delusions of grandeur for the children (for instance, thinking they can say "no" when told to clear the table – um, was a question even asked there?). In fact, I would submit that instead of moving us forward, the Democratic Parenting movement has set us back several steps.

How Democratic Parenting Is Letting Us Down: A Top-Ten List

1) **It's wasting our time.** As noted above, an unusually long amount of time can be spent attempting to explain to subordinates (children) why certain things just "are" (such as bedtimes, dental appointments, nutritious food, etc.) when a simple "Because I said so" takes less than four seconds. Try it.

2) **It's forcing us to redirect our energies.** We could be reading a book, chatting with a friend, or learning a new language. Instead, we are constantly forced to make sure

SITUATION	DEMOCRATIC RESPONSE	DEMOCRATIC RESULT	AUTOCRATIC RESPONSE	AUTOCRATIC RESULT
Fight between siblings over who gets the bigger piece of chocolate.	"Perhaps you two need to discuss whether it's the chocolate you want or a sense of real belonging in this family."	Long, drawn-out, boring fight that ultimately ends with a piece of chocolate being stuffed up someone's nose — an action driven by someone's sense of it really belonging there.	"Just take this piece and be happy you're getting anything."	Door slamming, kids crying, shouts of "It's not fair." Complete silence. Over in five minutes.
Kid asks a question for which Mom and/or or Dad don't have a feasible answer.	"I don't believe you have the Talking Stick right now, Jimmy. When it's your turn, Mommy will be sure to answer because I know you can handle sensitive adult information."	Long, drawn-out, boring discussion that ultimately ends with the child saying, "But you don't actually blow on it, right?"	"Because I said so."	Door slamming, kids crying, shouts of "It's not fair." Complete silence. Over in five minutes.
Family arguing over where to go on vacation.	"Let's have a family meeting tonight. We can all share our hopes and dreams for this amazing summer opportunity. But remember, the most important part is that we'll be together."	Long, drawn-out, boring discussion that ultimately ends with the kids saying, "Pick whatever you want, Mom and Dad, but just stop talking. I need to get to my friend's house."	"Mom and Dad will decide. We'll let you know what to pack. Here's a hint: Wherever we go, it will be licensed."	Trigger for further argument over who shares a bed with whom, who sits where in the car, etc. The fun never ends. Also, "Just because you have the money, you get to pick? No fair."* *Exactly.

that everyone's needs are met and that they are valued as human beings. Whatever.

3) **It's causing us to take our eye off the ball**. While we are at the organic-wood store shopping for a Talking Stick, we might be missing out on some valuable Facebook updates, Twitter gossip, and neighbors behaving badly – things all adults need to thrive.

4) **It raises false hopes**. The kids think they're equal to adults. In fact, they think they're equal to everyone. Then they get to school, and then work, and discover that they're at the bottom of the totem pole. Why let them go through that? Let them know they're there to begin with.

5) **It's creating monsters**. Children should not be in charge of planning a vacation, choosing dinner, selecting bedtimes, or deciding when to leave someone's house. This type of power will result in the contraction of a horrible disease, known as "entitlement," which is currently running rampant in North American society. You can't always get what you want, kids. Sometimes, you can't even get what you need.

6) **It leads to real-life avoidance**. It's pretty much guaranteed that someone is always going to be the boss of you, unless you're Richard Branson or Bill Gates. May as well face facts early: you're not in charge, kid.

7) **It fosters misguided beliefs**. Your voice is not equal. Your opinions are rarely valid. Get over it.

8) **It forces us to sweat the small stuff**. Determining whether your six-year-old is comfortable with the

decisions you've made regarding his bedroom decor undermines the fact that you bought and paid for the house that surrounds the bedroom he's living in. Get back to work and pay off that mortgage, and don't for a second reconsider changing that paint color.

9) **It's a slippery slope**. Once we let our children start making small decisions about what to have for dinner and what time they should go to bed, it's not long before they are successfully petitioning for the master bedroom and telling you that you can't have wine because you won't be able to drive them to a movie. And back. (Sorry about the scare tactics, but it needs to be said.)

10) **It's put bad thoughts in our heads**. The popularity of Democratic Parenting has somehow led us to believe that Autocratic Parenting (or, as it's known in nature, "real" parenting) is bad. Clearly some child was behind this theory in the first place.

Bottom line? It's pretty simple. I suggest you skip all of the talking, angst, and drama and embrace the fact that you can be the boss, just like in a successfully run business. Imagine! You can set the rules and make sure they are followed. You can listen to your kids without letting them run the show. Or you can waste time and energy letting them think that they are in charge and then figuring out ways to wrestle back some sense of control.

If you have the time to kill, go for it. But if you'd rather be more efficient and productive, you might want to consider laying down the law every once in a while. Because you can. You're. The. Boss.

FIVE WAYS IN WHICH AUTOCRATIC PARENTING RULES

Still having doubts? If even a small part of you isn't yet convinced that being the boss is the way to go, I'm clearly not making my point. Maybe it will help if we spend a bit of time exploring how and why Autocratic Parenting is so much better.

1) **R-E-S-P-E-C-T.** At the office, the minions/employees wouldn't dare question a superior in public or private. Why? They know the rules going in, and they are expected to abide by them. Where are the rules at home? An Autocratic Parent knows her non-negotiable rules and sticks to them, even if they're not written down on paper – which they should be by the time you finish reading this book.

2) **Roles and responsibilities** are clear in an autocratically parented household, just as they are in any corporation. Not living up to the expectations outlined in the job description? Stepping outside the bounds of the position? These scenarios are dealt with in a prescribed manner, after consulting some sort of employee handbook. You can do this at home too. And you should.

3) **Consequences** are known and acted upon. In the workplace, you're not likely to hear an employee say, "So what

are you going to do, fire me?" unless he means it. At home, children with delusions of power might be tempted to use the same words. With Democratic Parenting, you are helpless. With some simple management guiding principles, however, you can effectively demote an unsatisfactory employee.

4) **Clarity**. Everyone knows his or her place. The boss is at the top, and the children are at the bottom. Extra cake? We get it. Staying up late? We do, you don't. It's pretty straightforward. No confusion.

5) **Time efficiency**. We win every argument. In fact, there really aren't any arguments. We might once in a while look like we're listening, but we're really not. (Secret: I write grocery lists in my head when they talk.)

If you've been paying attention, you will know this: Boss equals good, anarchy equals bad. From the boardroom to the playroom, structure and a clear understanding of roles, responsibilities, and consequences (both good and bad) make for smoother experiences. The successful corporate model has been in front of us since before we had children. Allow the brain fog to clear and start fantasizing about a world where you are truly the boss of your own home. If you're still reading along,[5] you must be ready to take the plunge and to embrace the philosophy. Not sure how to

....

[5] And, duh, if you read that, you are. I'm smart like that.

apply it to your real life? Is it too late to go from being a sub-ordinate to your own children to truly running the show? It isn't. I'll show you how. Step by step.[6]

Most moms I know want and sometimes claim to be the "CEO of their family." That's terrific. Except most of them are not good or effective CEOs. They are CEOs in title only. They have not done the due diligence within their families to ensure that that their "team" has taken on the right respon-sibilities, established appropriate goals, and that everyone is clear in where they are going. This is a fundamental step in making sure you are an effective leader and not just another clichéd bad boss.

....

[6] You might want to open a spreadsheet to keep up.

REAL-LIFE LESSON

Between my first two years of university, I took a job as a reception-ist at a small firm that rented out . . . well, I'm not sure what they rented out. All I know is that I was quickly told that in addition to my "reception" duties (which admittedly were sparse as no one actually came into the office, hence there was no one to "receive"), I would be expected to make collection calls. "Sure!" I replied, having no idea that making calls for money is basically the worst job in the world . . . although as a student I was pretty good at making them to my parents, so I figured, How hard could it be?

Bear in mind this was in the mid-1980s, well before the preva-lence, if not invention of, caller ID. Everyone had a seven-digit land-line, and if you were lucky they might have a cassette-tape answering machine on the other end of the line. So I would pick up my huge coil-wire-anchored handset, dial in the number, and wait. On the rare occasion when someone answered the phone, they were never the right party (of course not!) and when they said they'd call me right back, I thought to myself how nice and polite they were. But, hey, they never called back, and at the end of the first week I was ready to pay off all their debts with my measly salary just so I didn't have to make any more calls. What did I learn? A few things: First, get a clear job description. Second, you're always going to have to do things you really don't like to do, regardless of your level of seniority. Third, it's hard to get money out of people. Also? If you're in a three-person office, about 1,000 square feet, and the boss has a shower in his office, be a little concerned.

KNOW THYSELF

Figuring Out the "Company" You Keep

Okay, so you've seen the light. You've even taken that light back from your child, who insisted on having it in her room. You're well on your way. You want to give being a boss at home a try. Congratulations on making a wise decision. By yourself. The way a real boss would – looking at all of the evidence, evaluating the best possible strategy for success, and implementing change to make it happen. *Thanks, Kathy,* you might be saying, *but what now? Management "theory" is one thing, but, really, where do I start?* First and foremost, you need to put your old ways of thinking out with the weekly trash.[7] Then you need to start thinking like the boss.

Imagine yourself as a newly hired CEO, showing up at the button factory/multinational oil conglomerate/ funky tech start-up for your first day of work. What's job number one? Firing the entire accounting department? Hiring your brother-in-law's best friend's second cousin

---

[7] On second thought, get your kids to take it out.

for that vacant spot in marketing? Maybe. Maybe not. But that's probably not the *first* thing you should do. The first thing you should do is get to know the company you've been charged with running. What are its assets and liabilities? Its core competencies? Its corporate culture? A good boss understands that knowledge is power. Without it, success of any kind is hard to achieve.

So, what kind of "company" are you the boss of and where do you want to take it? The answers to these questions need to come from the top (that's you, boss) and work their way down (to the kids, perhaps brushing up against a wayward husband en route). Let's find out where you are and where you want to go.

WHAT'S YOUR BRAND?

All companies have a brand, which is really just a fancy way of saying "personality." Remember those old commercials for Mac computers? There were two guys: one representing the Mac and one representing the PC. The Mac dude was funky, casual, adaptive, and young. The PC guy looked like your accountant on a bad day: stuffy, with old-school thinking, an inflexible nature, and a pocket protector. (Not that there's anything wrong with that.[8]) The

---

[8] My dad is an accountant. Hey, Dad!

point is that commercial played up the idea of corporate personality perfectly and left viewers with no doubt as to which computer was supposedly cool and which was considered outdated and a little stodgy.

Companies work hard to establish a brand and then make use of it. From a financial perspective, it helps them connect with potential consumers and, in turn, sell products. On a subtler level, it helps them establish goals and priorities and make decisions. They act in a way that makes sense from a brand perspective.

When it comes right down to it, families aren't so different. A family unit has a personality too, and knowing what your family is all about can help you make informed decisions about what is and is not important to the whole family unit and to you as the boss of that unit. Figuring out your family brand is a walk in the park when you take a cue or two from the corporate world.

Common Corporate and Family Brands: Anything Look Familiar?

So how does branding work on the home front? Let's take a quick look at some well-established brand personalities to see how they might translate in a family setting.

COMPANY	BRAND	FAMILY TRANSLATION
IBM	Trusted, secure, innovating within rules and secure strategies.	Parents with trusted jobs (accountant, teacher, dentist) and perfect children who always get school awards.

COMPANY	BRAND	FAMILY TRANSLATION
Yahoo!	Cutting edge with new thinking and always surprising and funky offices. Even hires women in top roles.	Working mom in high-profile career; stay-at-home dad who lets kids ride skateboards down busy roads.
Target	Good value while attempting to remain current through constant injections from new celebrity "designers."	Thrifty family that might have a budding artist erecting statues made out of recycled boxes on front lawn.

Are you getting the idea? The key thing to remember is that when it comes to family brands, the possibilities are endless. The three examples above barely scratch the surface. Each child can redefine a brand when he or she comes along. If you're feeling a bit stumped when it comes to categorizing your own motley crew, never fear. I've developed a handy multiple-choice quiz to help you sort it out.

Discover Your Family Brand

1) You've got ten minutes to feed the kids before throwing them in the minivan for drop off at three different hockey arenas. You:

    a) Pull out the wheat-germ loaf you made last month during your "Glucose-Free Living Bake-a-Thon to Support Organic Farmers" weekend, spread some homemade elderberry jam on top, and sprinkle with hemp seed.

    b) Actually, you don't own a minivan. You get the kids ready for a 10k ride on their bikes. They don't play hockey either. They are marathoners. And they ate energy bars a few minutes ago.

c) You pulled the kids out of hockey last year after you discovered the ancient sport of boar tossing during a recent family trip through Africa.

d) You threaten to cut off all electronics if they don't get their butts in the van in two minutes, you rip through a drive-thru and high-five your seven-year-old on discovering that you are the Customer of the Month. Again.

2) Your kid is fighting with another kid at school. You:

a) Advise your child not to pick on a child who is clearly weakened both physically and mentally by their white-bread, processed-sugar, and high-fat diet.

b) Try to divert their energy by organizing a marathon to raise money for children who don't have use of their arms . . . to fight with.

c) Train your child in the ancient sport of boar tossing.

d) Tell your kid to suck it up and then make passive-aggressive remarks to the other kid's mom. Gossip about the entire family behind their back.

3) Your children refuse to go to and stay in bed. You:

a) Eliminate all sugar from their diet. That should work.

b) Redirect their energies into harnessing power through the exercise bike you have connected to your windmill.

c) Accept that the jetlag your children constantly experience is a symbol of how you have chosen to expose them to the wonders of the world. Embrace this.

d) Tell them if they don't get their butts in bed by the time you count to three, you'll make them sleep in the basement next to the empty wine cellar. Where zombies live.

4) You and your teenage daughter can't agree on what constitutes suitable clothing for her to wear to school. You tell her:

a) That if a hemp sack dress is good enough for you, it's good enough for her. It's what's on the inside that counts.

b) There is nothing wrong with wearing a shirt that has been passed down from her three older brothers. And does she really want to kill a cow just to get a leather coat? (Make her watch that video, again.)

c) While it may be fine for Caribbean stage performers to wear feathers and bikinis made of pearls like you saw last week, no, you don't think Daisy Dukes, feather earrings, and a tube top are a good North American interpretation.

d) Cut off her allowance, take her shopping at DrabMoms R Us, and tell her if you catch her rolling up her T-shirt again you'll take away her iPhone.

5) Your four-year-old insists on watching the same episode of *Caillou*, over and over again. You:

a) Distract him with a lovely piece of kale-and-quinoa loaf. And then chart his transit time.

b) Please. You don't own a TV and if you accidentally did, you wouldn't let your child watch anything other than educational programs and documentaries.

c) Make him do jumping jacks while watching the show in order to keep his body activated even when his mind isn't.

d) Tell him if you have to watch one more minute of that whiny brat you'll wash his hair with the same shampoo that Caillou's mom used. What hair? Exactly.

Scoring:

A: If you answered mostly A, you clearly have nutrition and organic food at the top of your priority list. Your kids are healthy and skinny and have zero sense of humor.

B: If you answered mostly B, your commitment to the environment and attempts to be socially responsible should be commended.[9] But not with a plaque made from new raw materials.

C: If you answered mostly C, you have decided that the world is your classroom. Your ability to look down your nose at your commonplace North American counterparts is world class.

D: If you answered mostly D, congratulations on being honest, sister! Cheers!

....

[9] Chances are you're no fun. Sorry.

Family Brands to Avoid Like the Plague

We all know that expression "There's no such thing as bad PR." Actually, there is. (Remember Michael Richards?) And bad public relations around your family can haunt you for years at a school, in a neighborhood, or during get-togethers with relatives. Some family branding and publicity should be avoided at all costs. If you think you are leaning toward any of these family-branding stereotypes, you might want to re-evaluate your strategic plan.

- **Yelling Family**: One of my personal favorites – the screeching mom, the angry teenagers, the loud bursts of a daddy baritone . . . love these guys. They make the rest of us feel civil and proud. Yell on, fine people.

- **Late Family**: No matter what you are expecting them for – school, a wedding, a family gathering, a dinner party, or picking up your kid for hockey – these folks simply *cannot* arrive anywhere on time. You've tried, oh you've tried. Telling them to set their clock fifteen minutes ahead, giving them a time a half an hour ahead of when they really need to be somewhere (that works once, then they're on to you), buying them diaries, day planners, alarms . . . nothing works. This is their lifestyle. If you happen to know a Late Family, you'll have to adapt and carry on, and don't rely on them to bring appetizers to a potluck or save seats for you at the movies. As for your own family brand, you don't want to adopt this, trust me. Everyone will be mad at you, always. Are you reading this, Late People?

- **Disaster Family**: This is the family who always manages to have at least one member fall sick or get injured on a vacation; routinely has something blow up, get wet, or collapse in their house; and has the best excuses for missing school concerts (the bulldozer drove through our basement), parent-teacher interviews (the water line to the fridge exploded in my face), or the last game of the hockey playoffs (the back tire just flew off as we drove down the highway). Don't try to compete. They will always have a better/worse story. They are "toppers"; folks whose story has to top someone else's, all the time. "You twisted your ankle in Hamilton? I went across Europe with a broken foot." So. There's that. Steer clear. And do everything in your power not to be these people. Even when bad things happen, try not to talk about it too much. Particularly on social media or around people who might want to give you work.[10]

Okay, now you have a clear picture in your mind of what your brand should be or, more importantly, shouldn't be. Before we talk about how to put this newfound information to work, we need to lock in one more piece of the puzzle.

....

[10] It makes you seem incompetent, and incompetency is not a valued employee or consultant attribute.

BRAND EXTENSION: THE MISSION STATEMENT

The next time you visit a corporate website, look at the "About Us" page. Most feature a mission statement,[11] a few sentences or paragraphs that tell the world at large what the company does and what it wants to accomplish.

I have a theory about mission statements. I believe that they came to be as a result of countless CEOs asking countless versions of the same question: What am I trying to accomplish here? And how many times might you have muttered this yourself as a mother? While literally or figuratively pounding your head against the wall? The mission statement is a shortcut to the answer – a handy-dandy, quick-reference guide to what the company is all about. Or why you chose to throw birth-control caution to the wind. Once or twice.[12]

The idea of applying a mission statement to life on the home front isn't new. In fact, I'm pretty sure some Democratic Parent somewhere advised families to develop a mission statement and stick to it. The idea was probably conceived at a family meeting, where everyone had a turn with the Talking Stick. Sigh. Try to put that image out of your mind and focus on the end, not the means. As the boss of your family, you will likely find a mission statement handy, if for no other

....

[11] If you can't find this, be a little concerned that this company doesn't know what it's doing. Or the people running it are very, very smart. Who knows?

[12] Or four times. What was I thinking? Cue more head pounding.

reason than to remind yourself of what you were thinking when you brought these people into the world. And why you shouldn't take them out. You can use a mission statement for your own autocratic purposes. Corporately, a mission statement should address the employees, the shareholders, and the customers. It has to. If one of the stool's three legs isn't in place, the whole thing falls apart and you end up on the floor on your butt. To avoid that embarrassing and potentially painful situation, here's a quick primer on adapting those three categories to family life.

- **Employees:** This one's easy – or it should be after reading this far! Your employees are the members of your family. And we all know who the boss is, right? Reread the title of this book if you have to.
- **Shareholders:** This refers to your own parents – or any other relative or friend who has invested in you and wants you to be successful. No matter how old you are, your parents will always want to take responsibility for your successes and your failures. If you are the parent of a young child and currently wondering when things get easier, it sucks to realize this. There is, however, an upside. After an appearance I had on a national television show, my mother received an e-mail from a friend. It read: "You must be very proud of her." I'm forty-nine, but I'll take it.
- **Customers:** Hmm, tricky. We're not selling anything, are we? Or are we? Think about that for a minute and maybe rephrase the question. Who are we getting to buy

from us? Our neighbors, friends, acquaintances? Everyone we interact with on a daily basis? How about the world at large? Yes, let's go with that.

All right, let's get started. At its most basic level, a mission statement should easily and clearly define who you are and what you do. Think of it as your family's elevator speech. In case you're not familiar with that particular bit of corporate speak, an elevator speech is a thirty-second-or-less summary of what your business is – thirty seconds being the amount of time you might have someone trapped with you in an elevator on its way to the higher floor, where the execs hang out. In kid terms, this might be the time you've got to introduce yourself at an indoor playground before the screaming starts.

Let's look at a few world-class mission statements and see how they might be adapted for use by your family.

Avon

Leader in Global Beauty: *Build a unique portfolio of beauty and related brands, striving to surpass competitors in quality, innovation, and value, and elevating Avon's image to become the world's most trusted beauty company.*

Quality, innovation, and value. And here I thought they were out to paper the world with their catalogues and provide a measly income for stay-at-home moms! I sold Avon when I was in between jobs in Calgary. I didn't make much money, but it did provide me with something of value. I got fresh air and exercise (with my two kids in a double stroller), and it gave me something to do outside of the house. The experience also helped me realize what I didn't want to do. Perhaps *that* could be a part of a family mission statement. Know what you want to do, and add value.

Chevron

At the heart of The Chevron Way is our vision . . . to be the global energy company most admired for its people, partnership and performance.

I love this one. The word *admired* is strong and implies that the company acts with integrity and has great success. I'd like to put the word *admired* in my own family mission statement. Know what you want, add value, and be admired for it. Let's keep going.

General Motors

GM is a multinational corporation engaged in socially responsible operations, worldwide. It is dedicated to providing products and services of such quality that our customers will receive superior value while our employees and business partners will share in our success and our stock-holders will receive a sustained superior return on their investment.

What I find most interesting about GM's mission statement is the fact that they don't specifically state what their products and services actually are; rather, they put the focus on being socially responsible and providing value. There's the word *value* again.

Guess Who?

There's another company that goes even further than GM in terms of making the product (or service) less important than the experience of the customer (or employees, shareholders, fellow earth inhabitants, etc.). Do you know whose mission (they don't use the word *statement*) this is?

- *To refresh the world . . .*
- *To inspire moments of optimism . . .*
- *To create value and make a difference.*

They'd also like to teach the world to sing and are partial to polar bears. Yep, you guessed it: this is Coca-Cola. In both GM and Coke we see that what we are producing is less important than how we are producing it and what the impact on the world will be. This can certainly work in a family context. We're at "Know what you want, add value, and be admired for it." Let's revise that now to say, "Know what you want, add value, be admired for it, and provide inspiration."

Now it's your turn. Poke around on the Internet and do some research. Make a list of words that mean something to you, that perhaps reflect the attitudes or approaches you feel are important: commitment, knowledge, quality, weight loss, child control, or wherever your focus needs to be. String the ideas together until you come up with a mission statement of your own. Mine? I worked with keywords such as *know, admire, inspire, value, personal mastery,* and *focus.*

After a lot of thought, I boiled it down to this: "Do your best. People are watching."

Words to live by, pretty much in any context.

USING THE BRAND

Knowing what your brand is and establishing a clear and actionable mission statement gives successful companies the self-knowledge they need to accomplish their goals. It gives them power in the corporate world. The good news? We can do this at home as well. Still not clear? Here are some practical examples of how the boss at home can use this clearer sense of who and what the "company" is all about.

To Get Some Things Done

Let's say your mission statement is "Cleanliness at any cost."[13] Kids leaving half-empty milk glasses on the kitchen table? Unmade beds? Shoes in the front hall? A little reminder about what your mission is can work wonders. (It's important to focus on the mission statement here and not the fact that Mom might be a tad anal.)

Other examples might include "Tuned to success" (television watching is just fine with this family), "Providing quality meals at affordable prices" (better embrace that

---

[13] I don't know who this might be, but there are delusional folks out there who think a house can be full of children and clean. Hahahahaha!

tuna casserole, kids), or "Kids are people too!" (the type of people who have to vacuum, do laundry, and sweep every once in a while).

To Avoid Doing Some Things

Mission statements can also be deployed to avoid doing certain things that don't fit with the boss's perception of the family or that Mom (I mean, the boss) doesn't want to do. "Broken bones be barred," for example, would be a good way to get out of making the trip across town to the skateboard park. "Supporting the independent strength of others" is useful when looking for an excuse not to help out with your child's homework.[14] Something as simple as "Saying no to noxious fumes" gets you out of driving your children. Anywhere.

Branding? Check. Mission statement? Done. Now it's time to deploy these corporate must-haves within the confines of your home's walls. And on the little people who live there. I know they say that people are a company's most valuable asset,[15] but they could be your worst nightmare. I guess it depends on the people. Speaking of which . . . who are yours? That's our next step.

....

[14] Which, frankly, after grade five, you couldn't do if you tried.
[15] Every company says it. Even when they're "right-sizing" you out of your job. It's for the best, really.

REAL-LIFE LESSON

Sometimes I just do things without really knowing how to do them. Luckily, my own personal mission statement is "Sure, I can do that!" Like the time I decided to open up my own baby-and-maternity consignment store. The fact that I had a twenty-month-old, was pregnant with my second, and had no retail-store management experience whatsoever seemed like tiny details. I had just moved to Calgary and wasn't planning on opening a store immediately, but circumstances developed that required me to move up my plan by a full year. So I hauled my bloated self into the Alberta Treasury Branch and confidently filled out a small-business loan application, for all of $2,000. I visited auctions for store fixtures and racking, tacked up signs all over town looking for inventory, and dragged my toddler from accountants to lawyers to sign makers to printers until I was ready to take a break. It was all in line with my mission statement. My due date came and I (of course!) was on time, so I took two weeks off after the birth (a lovely boy named Alexander[16]) and then launched back in. Five weeks after I had given birth, the store Baby Baby opened to rave reviews. Well, not rave reviews per se, but the ravings of my now two-year-old as she fought off the other kids in *her* store play area.

With the name of the store being Baby Baby, most people assumed I was in the business of selling baby clothing/goods. Not, however, the radio DJ who called me one morning asking if I had anything naughty to sell him. On the air. Perhaps I should have thought through my branding just a little better, or established a sideline.

....

[16] Now nineteen years old. Crazy. I mean his age, not him.

GET YOUR DUCKS IN A ROW

Sorting Out the "Staff"

One of the first things an effective boss does is get to know his or her staff. Understanding their strengths and weaknesses, whether or not they're in a role that suits them, is crucial when it comes to the success of the business. The same is true on the home front. We can make sure that roles and responsibilities are understood and that we are taking full advantage of everyone's talents, for our own benefit.

In the workplace, all of this is governed by organizational charts, job descriptions, roles-and-responsibilities tables, and a clear understanding of who does what.

Do you know what all of these things have in common? Every single one – every policy, procedure, and workflow spreadsheet – starts and ends in the human resources department. So what's the equivalent at home? You guessed it. That would be you, Mom. Don't tell me you're surprised by this! We're human *and* we're resourceful.[17] As you embark

---

[17] Which is more than I can say for some dads.

on your quest to become the efficient and effective boss of your own family, it may help to understand a bit more about the HR world. It has its own unique concerns and often its own language (see Step 8: Have Fun for more on that). Everything from the initial hire (i.e., birth) to the final firing (hopefully college, or at least that first job, before the age twenty-five – whatever comes first) needs to be considered. Here's a hint: Not all employees are star employees all of the time. Some are not even star employees *some* of the time. In an office, human resource policies are put in place to ensure that all employees are treated fairly. Now wouldn't that be an amazing thing to achieve in your house? (Don't worry: just like at the office, you don't actually have to treat them fairly; they just need to think that you are.)

If kids are like employees – and haven't we established that they are? – they have to be nurtured, trained, and developed. Like everything to do with parenting, these specific activities are expensive and time consuming. But as the boss, you are responsible. If you need some motivation, consider this: The boss's job becomes much easier if the employees are well managed and satisfied. So how, exactly, is a mom supposed to achieve this? It all starts with a little organization.

WHO'S ON TOP?

A pecking order is always a good thing; it helps keep things civil and, mostly, running smoothly. Only in the cartoon world of *SpongeBob Squarepants* does the bottom-of-the-food-chain creature, Plankton, have any control. And it never works out for him.[18] Nature loves a natural order of species, as should an organized family.

In most offices, we don't actually witness the lioness perched over the zebra carcass. Instead, we have an organizational chart. There was a period in the late 1980s when "matrix management" was all the rage, and human resource specialists everywhere went a little crazy trying to get everyone's boxes on the same line, but the top-down method continues to be the key to success.

This same strategy can easily be applied on the home front. I mean, let's be clear about who's in charge, shall we?

Your Very Own Organization

To get us started, let's imagine a typical business model as shown opposite:

Pretty easy to figure out who's on top, what the reporting structure is, and what areas of responsibility are being covered by whom.

So who's on top at home? That's right . . . you. The boss. Then what? Do you have a middle manager (I'm thinking maybe Dad . . . maybe)? Is he ready for that role? How many kids are "in play"? They're probably all junior employees, unless you have a teenager. Although these teen employees

....

[18] Yes, I watch the show enough to know of Plankton's foibles. So?

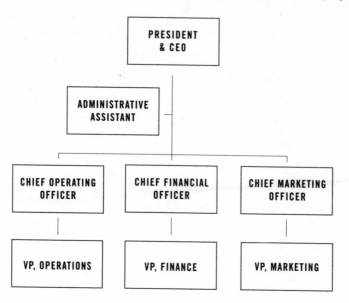

are a bit higher up the food chain, they come with their own challenges, from a managerial perspective (more on that later). Here's how a family organizational chart might look:

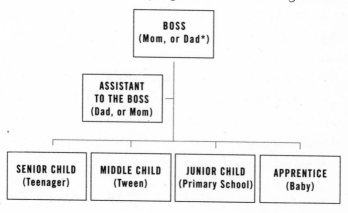

*OK, it's Mom.

Now, you may be wondering why all of my "direct reports" are on the same line, no matter what their age/experience. It's because they all, by definition, report directly to *me*. The Boss. Not to each other, as some teenagers might think. (For example, "You're not allowed to sit there. That's *my* spot." Um . . . no, it's not.) Interestingly, siblings are not only permitted to say, "You are so not the boss of me" to each other, they are encouraged to do so. This keeps the boss–employee continuum and understanding balanced. They are, after all, co-workers.[19]

Chain of Command

Now that you've got your handy-dandy organization chart all complete and tacked to the fridge, you've also got . . . wait for it . . . a reporting structure! This is clearly outlined in the org chart – and everyone reports to you, so really, how hard is it? But how often do they report and about what? The answers to these questions are essential when it comes to having an organization and/or family run successfully. What are your subordinates expected to consult with you on, and what can they accomplish themselves? It's helpful to sort these things out in the early going so, like at the office, there are no misunderstandings. You don't want to be the last to know about:

- the phone call that's coming in from the principal. You'll need time beforehand to prepare/punish;

....

[19] The actual word *work* being open to interpretation with these guys, of course.

- your son and that woman's son getting caught jumping on logs at the park in their underwear (It has to be that other kids' fault somehow.); and
- the end-of-soccer-season party your husband agreed to host. That he won't be able to attend.

On the other hand, you decidedly don't want to know:

- every time a certain someone's stupid brother says or does something stupid (He's your kid too. You know perfectly well what he's up to.);
- that your husband took the garbage out. Oh, he has to do it, but he doesn't have to announce it each and every time. But he does; and
- about the dead mouse in the basement. Someone just needs to clean that up and never speak of it again.

Establishing roles and responsibilities within your reporting structure is essential to keeping a tight ship afloat and, of course, to keeping the things you need to know on a need-to-know basis.[20]

---

[20] Nose-picking siblings. Don't need to know. Really.

JOB DESCRIPTIONS FOR THE LITTLE PEOPLE[21]

The next logical step on the road to managerial bliss is the creation of job descriptions. Why is this blissful? Because once you have something written down on paper you can point to it every time the kids question your authority.[22] That's what they do in an office, and it seems to work pretty well in terms of shutting down further conversation (which is, after all, a basic management pillar). Job descriptions are necessary so that managers know who to praise when things are going well and, more importantly, who to blame when projects go off the rails or, at home, when the toddler has access to Mommy's mascara. Establishing clear expectations and making sure you are all on the same page (even if some of you can't read yet) will pave the road for smoother execution of everything from boring old domestic chores to reminding certain people that deciding what to eat for dinner or where they get to sit in the car is not part of their responsibilities.

Why not start by writing your own job description, and don't forget that recognizing what you *don't* want to do is just as important as recognizing what you do want to do.

....

[21] They really are little people, so this isn't meant to be at all derogatory – just a bit condescending.
[22] And maybe an errant husband.

Title: The Boss

Role: To ensure the smooth running of the household.

Responsibilities:

1) Ensuring that you have the same number of children under your care at the end of the day as when you started.[23]

2) Managing and delegating household duties, including but not limited to garbage collection, vacuuming, laundry, groceries, wiping, sweeping, brushing, shining and polishing anything that doesn't have a pulse. And some things that do.

3) Serving as the final decision maker on bed times, meal times, meal ingredients, nutritional requirements being met for the day, acceptable state of cleanliness for clothing and faces, hair cut appropriateness, and tattoo approval.[24]

---

[23] With the possible exception of that neighborhood kid who always seems to be here for a meal and sleepover. Doesn't he have a home?

[24] It ain't ever coming, so don't hold your breath on this one, kids.

Title: Assistant to the Boss
Role: Enforcing whatever the boss says[25]
Responsibilities:

1) Developing the automatic response of "Listen to your mother" unless you have previously been delegated as the final decision maker and/or laborer for a child's request.[26]
2) That wine rack? Stock it.

Title: Senior Child (Teenager)
Role: Knowing better
Responsibilities:

1) Not showing attitude through eye-rolling, sighing, rude hand gestures, or mad texting to sibling sitting next to you at the dinner table (yes, we see that).
2) Doing things to help, not hinder, your younger siblings, including but not limited to not poking them every time they walk past or holding their stuffies for ransom.
3) Just smarten up.

....

[25] Yes, dear.
[26] Please note that you may be required to know which scenario is in play without specifically being told by the boss. You're just supposed to know what you are supposed to do. Is that too much to ask? Really? Did you give birth? Okay then.

Title: Middle Child (Tween)

Role: To take on only the socially acceptable qualities of the senior child and ignore the rest

Responsibilities:

1) Not growing up too quickly and missing the part where you're big enough to be helpful and helpful enough to be big.

2) Not wearing age-inappropriate clothing before its time, or in front of the boss.

3) Letting your guard down enough to sneak in one last pre-teen snuggle – after learning about the importance of personal hygiene.

Title: Junior Child (Primary-School Age)

Role: Not questioning authority

Responsibilities:

1) Dressing, cleaning, and bathing yourself.

2) That's about it.

Title: Apprentice (Baby/Toddler)

Role: Birth control reminder

Responsibilities:

1) Eating, sleeping, pooping.

2) Repeat.

You've got the hang of this now, right? So go ahead and write job descriptions for your own brood. You know your kids better than anyone else. What do you want them to do? What are they currently capable of doing? What should they be striving for over the days and months to come? Remember, none of this is carved in stone. Job descriptions – both corporate and family – can and should be revised on a regular basis. People and circumstances change all the time. A good boss knows how to adapt.

FOLLOW THROUGH: THE PERFORMANCE REVIEW

If you're really following along here, you've now laid out specific tasks in your children's and husband's job descriptions – clearing the table, making beds, mowing the lawn – all good things. But what's the point of this unless you have a plan for dealing with (dare I say it) failure? Yes, even children born after 1990 can fail (or be "success challenged"), although they and their Helicopter (enabling) Parents will never admit it.

At work, when expectations aren't met, the employee is taken to task during the dreaded yearly performance review. This is basically a meeting where the boss gets to tell the employee all the ways in which she isn't getting the job done (and maybe a couple of the ways she is), and the employee gets to tell the boss why she should be: a) earning more money and b) sporting a better title. The key to a successful performance review, from a boss's perspective, is that nobody cries and expectations for the following quarter are fully understood. You might even want to throw your employee a bone every six months or so by upgrading her title with a well-placed "coordinator" or "associate" designation where appropriate.

It works this way at home too. Schedule a meeting, one on one, with your "staff." I find this works better if they don't even realize they're in a performance review meeting. They just think you've just miraculously changed your mind last minute and have agreed to drive them downtown to a concert. Really, you have them trapped in the car and in a good frame of mind to hear some home truths. Start by telling them everything they've done right (make some up if you have to: "I love the way you don't jostle the table when you sit down for dinner") and then let them have it.[27]

Before you begin, it's worth reminding yourself that the performance review is a one-way piece of communication – always has been corporately and will remain so at home. The superiors get to rate the subordinates. That's why we're superior. Get it? (Read the title of the book again if you have to.) And while it can be a little fun to make a cocky junior product manager cry (come on, admit it) in a performance review, you don't want to traumatize your children in the same way.[28] Remember these words from author

....

[27] In this situation, they'll still want to get to the concert, so they might be willing to rein in some of that defensive attitude they usually dish out. Always thinking, right?
[28] Not really. Unless you're PMSing. Defensible then.

Judith Martin ("Miss Manners") if you find yourself struggling through the "accomplishments" section with certain children: "If you can't be kind, at least be vague."

Not sure how to get started? Here's a template performance review form, filled out to help you get the idea.

PERFORMANCE REVIEW

Employee Name:_____Sarah_____

Age at Time of Review:_____7 ¾_____

Position:_____Youngest

___X___Middle

_____Oldest

_____Only*

*Never mind, you win. Go buy yourself a pony.

Basic Job Responsibilities: Getting dressed for school and not sitting on the baby.

Annual Goals:

1. Passing other family members in hall/kitchen/bathroom/ mudroom without smirking, smacking, or sniggering.
2. Not allowing any dirty clothes to land on the carpet, in any room.
3. Abandoning attempt to break record in "days in same underwear" competition.

Rated Qualities: On a scale of 1 to 4, with 1 being "Did I bring the wrong kid home from the hospital?" and 4 being "It must be my good parenting."

__2__ Attitude*   __4__ Hygiene   __2__ Smart-assedness

__2__ Clutter   __3__ Scholastic   __1__ Visits to principal

__1__ Participation in school plays/concerts**

__3__ Harm to Mom & Dad's vocal chords

__4__ Depletion of therapy fund

*Adjusted during teenage years; be reasonable.

** Please note that there is a level (i.e., >1) at which this becomes a derogatory.

Overall Rating: __2.5__

Scores:

0 Chances are, you're getting in trouble right now and don't even have time to read this.

1 Smarten up. There's only so much money in the therapy fund. For Mom.

2 You had one bright spot. Work on that, stop hitting your brother, and pick up that underwear you wore for three days.

3 You're an angel at school but more "yourself" at home. How about pretending you're at school all the time?

4 Pretty much perfect. You know how to explain your transgressions and constantly give yourself a slightly less-worse edge over the sibling annoying someone in front of you. Well done.

5 While there is undoubtedly some butt-kissing going on here, we enjoy that and look forward to your future endeavors. On a negative note, your good behavior has likely caused issues for another child, so your allowance will be docked in order to pay for their testing and subsequent medication. Mom's too.

Promotability:[29]___No___. While Sarah shows excellent promise as a grade-two student – not overly involved in school activities – her inclination to pick scabs and eat them needs to be examined in more detail. By someone else.

This is all well and good if you have a model employee like Sarah here, but what if things aren't going so well? If you find that your direct reports are continually letting you down in terms of meeting expectations, you want to have a system of probation and, ultimately, punishment in place just like they do in the work world.

PROBATION

In a corporate setting, if an employee's goals and objectives are not met, a litigiously aware firm will put said employee through a series of probationary periods, during which they are expected to provide extra reporting and endure increased scrutiny. This can also be implemented at home. Here's how it works:

- Teen breaks curfew. Teen loses right to be out for a set period of time, say, two weeks (old-school term for this: *grounding*).
- Daughter spends gas money on new shirt. Daughter loses right to use car, or wear new shirt, for a set period of time

....

[29] Yes or no will do. It's arbitrary anyway. Don't worry about it. Most companies don't either.

(or until Mom can determine whether the shirt works better for her and is willing to give up her car again).

- Ten-year-old son and friend decide to re-enact a scene from Minecraft using bricks from the garden. In the basement. Son loses right to see friend for a set period of time. Unless that friend's mom decides to invite your son for a sleepover. Really, who are you punishing by not sending him?

Get the idea? And doesn't *probation* sound both more professional and punitive than the words *time-out* or *grounded* that parents have deployed in the past? If you're still balking at the idea, remember this: Not only is having an unhappy child okay, it can be totally beneficial. We can find out what makes our children unhappy and then use it to punish them. This isn't as mean as you might think. I could send one of my kids to her room for a time-out when she's misbehaved and she would actually love it. Quiet time with a book, away from stinky brothers . . . it's all good. But another one of my kids hates peace and quiet and being away from the crowd. Forget finding the punishment to suit the crime; find the punishment to fit the child.

Are you seeing the light here? The great thing about a top-down management system is that the boss can take punitive action if so required. Some parenting experts, such as Alyson Schafer,[30] call this "punitive parenting." In fact, it was Alyson

---

[30] Parenting expert, psychotherapist, and good friend. Also a fun debate partner on Autocratic versus Democratic Parenting!

who taught me the expression, although she said it like it was a bad thing. Punitive parenting is basically a system that uses more of a stick than a carrot when it comes to modifying children's behavior. It has been my experience that children generally like sticks better than carrots anyway.

Of course I don't condone child abuse, verbal or physical, but there was something to be said for the way my parents punished me and my siblings. Anyone else out there get a twinge of fear when they see a wooden spoon or a hair brush? Punishment today, if we're even allowed to call it that, let alone execute it, is supposed to be a series of "teaching moments" and "self-discovery" geared toward encouraging our kids to discover for themselves why what they did was wrong. Wait, did I say "wrong"? Not sure that's even allowed. They're never wrong, are they?

In the work world, if an employee does something egregious or not up to scratch, at a minimum it's kept on record for their annual performance review and at worst it can result in firing. You can't fire your kids (at least I haven't figured out how), but you can certainly let them know that they can do better.

PROMOTIONS

All right. Enough about punishments. Let's turn our attention to a much less common scenario. You may have noticed the "promotability" line in the sample performance review form. You may be thinking, *Is she crazy? You can't promote your children.* Wanna bet?

While you can't make a middle child the oldest, or grant a twelve-year-old the privileges of a sixteen-year-old, you can find ways to reward them through promoted benefits within the household. This can take the form of greater responsibility and greater rewards.

- **Promotable Action**: Homework finished on time, without whining, and they didn't ask you once to check it or stump you with a question you didn't know the answer to. **Promotion**: They take on role of Chief Dinner Adviser for the rest of the week and share in the choosing (and preparation, if they want) of the family meal. Selecting dishes particularly hated by siblings makes this a popular promotion to achieve.
- **Promotable Action**: Helping with setting and clearing the table, without being asked or demanding monetary compensation. **Promotion**: They are awarded the title of Senior Management, Media Control for the evening and are responsible for selecting programs to be shown on the best television in the house.[31]
- **Promotable Action**: Taking out the garbage and putting the garbage and recycling cans away after they've been emptied without being nagged more than once.

---

[31] Please note that parents are not required to watch said programming, particularly if it involves the word *glee*.

Promotion: They are awarded Hallway Monitor status and can leave their knapsacks and shoes strewn in the front hallway for a week while demanding that others put theirs away.[32]

When discussing the concept of promotion with your children, you will want to stress the rewards part and downplay the responsibility part. Do this right and it will work out well for everyone. Kids will always ask for extra "benefits" (e.g., a later bedtime[33]) without doing the work to show they're responsible enough to handle new levels of entitlement. This is why the performance review is so valuable: you can use it to make them prove that they deserve it (whatever "it" might be) – to both you and to themselves.

Assessing Promotability at Home

In an office environment, one of the biggest challenges a manager can face is who to promote and when. As someone who once managed a twenty-person team, I can tell you this: the ones who are promotable rise quickly to the top. Is it their ability? Yes. Is it their attitude? Absolutely. Is it their enthusiasm? For me, this is the most important quality. Be enthusiastic. The old saying "there are no small jobs" (adapted from "there are no small parts, just small actors")

....

[32] Excluding Mom and Dad.
[33] If your child does not have an established bedtime, stop reading this right now and set one. Use a timer if you have to.

is really true. Enthusiastic employees take on the smallest of tasks. Not only do they do them exceedingly well, they often find better ways to complete the job, and they do it with a smile on their face. If an employee is constantly whining about his responsibilities, or unable to get his job done, he's in the wrong job. It's as simple as that.

I remember "inheriting" an employee onto a team, a girl who on paper had it made (the MBA, the strong corporate background), but the last thing she wanted to do was work in the world of corporate marketing. She wanted to be a photographer, but her family had pushed her into this role.[34] Quite frankly, she was pretty bad at it. But instead of managing her out, her former bosses had kept her in a junior-level job (which she was competent at) and passed her over for promotion, pushing ahead younger and less-experienced people. She was known on the management team as a "Lifer Product Manager." How awful. During my first performance review with her, I looked her in the eye and said, "You can't be enjoying this, can you?" She said, "No." But as the work she had done was adequate, I couldn't fire her. And she didn't quit. And so what did I do? What would most managers in this position do? I gave her a ringing endorsement when she applied for a job in another department, just to get rid of her.[35]

....

[34] I spoke with David Chilton (author of *The Wealthy Barber*) recently, and he said one of the biggest financial regrets people have today is the cost of their university education, if they didn't need it for a specific profession, of course. Don't push your kids into an educational stream for a job they'll never like, or maybe even get. No one wins. Especially their employer.
[35] So far, attempts to transfer underperforming children to other families has failed, FYI.

How do enthusiasm, an overall good attitude, and love of the "job" play out on the home front? In much the same way as they do in the office, as it turns out. It's unfortunate that your lunch bag got left in the back of the vehicle Dad took in today to get new tires, but I think not sliding off the road and dying in a fiery crash is more important than any embarrassment that might be caused by you having to use a plastic shopping bag for your lunch today. Smiles all around? Turn that frown upside down, mister!

So what other qualities can we look for when assessing promotability? The same qualities you want to see your children displaying as you are raising them to be responsible, decent, and salary-earning individuals. That's not a typo. They're not going to earn a good salary without displaying:

- **Willingness to learn**. This is associated with attitude, for sure, but it's slightly different. Some employees can have a great attitude about their current work and life situations but totally put the brakes on when it comes to doing anything even slightly outside their comfort zone. Keep pushing forward. The kid who has mastered putting herself to bed now has to embrace keeping that damn light off all night long.
- **Empathy and support**. At some point, we all need to learn that someone else's success does not take away from our own. It's not a zero-sum game. Yet as kids, we all seem to start off with this assumption: "Hey, he gets to go to the all-star game with Dad and I don't? That sucks. Not fair!" First of all, life isn't fair. Second, we're not stupid.

We will do our best to even things out, *if* you support the success and luck (yes, I said luck) of others. Listen up, kids: you don't have to be sincere in the flattery of your siblings, but there is a time and a place for false compliments and faked good humor. And not just at home. I am astounded daily by the petty jealousies and nastiness I see on Twitter when a fellow tweep is rewarded with success. We're watching. You're being childish. Like my actual children. Fake some enthusiasm, okay?

- **Appearance**. How you dress, comb your hair, wash your face . . . it all matters for a kid trying to make a good impression, and it really matters when you're an adult. Take care of yourself or others won't believe that you can take care of their business. I know many teenage girls who go out in public in their pajama pants and belly shirts – not only to school, but also to that first babysitting job. Moms don't generally trust teen girls in bellyshirts to make good decisions about their children, BTW.

The promotion of someone into a new position – complete with greater responsibility – is just as much, if not more, a reflection of the supervising manager's abilities as it is of the promotee's skill set. No one wants to back a loser. We don't so much want to parent one either.

Assessing Seniority

Before we leave the happy land of promotions, there's one more thing you might want consider, as the boss and all. Say you've sorted out that junior employees one through three are all ripe and ready for a promotion. Great! Well done, boss. As children get older, so their responsibility in the home and, most importantly, *for themselves* can grow. Yes, I'm pretty sure that a nineteen-year-old can go to a dentist appointment by himself. As employees take on more responsibility and are seen as being more senior, the burden on the boss shrinks. "Seniority" is a long sought-after goal in the corporate world. This needs to be the same ideal at home.

But hold off for just a minute on revising the job descriptions. Have you considered the added complication of how to know exactly which "employee" has the most seniority (it's not as easy as checking their birth certificates)? The oldest child doesn't necessarily make for the most competent worker, but birth order does have a huge amount to do with who they are and how they respond to orders and responsibilities.

The Oldest

The oldest child is often a bit of a prima donna (check with your friends; I think you'll see this is mostly true), the original model, the gold standard for the children who will follow. May also be spoiled, temperamental, and used to having his or her own way.[36] Eldests are also charged with more responsibility than their younger siblings and can find themselves taking on more adult responsibilities as the team grows larger. They will

....

[36] To my older sister — just kidding!

often grow to resent being the parental assistant. The plus side? They will also be prepared to take on responsibility sooner and will be quick to point out when those younger than them are transgressing. This takes some of the burden off of Mom.

The Middle Child

The poor, overlooked, and ignored middle child. At least that's what every middle child and family-oriented TV program would have you believe. As a middle child, I think it's a pretty sweet spot. The trail has been blazed by the older child (who still gets stuck with the most responsibility), so Mr. or Ms. Center Square can kick back and relax while his or her older sibling works hard and the baby of the family gets fawned over. Never underestimate the benefits of flying under the radar; it allows you to set your own path. As the manager, you can use this to your advantage, since middle children are far more likely to appreciate attention when they get it. Pointing out your middle child's good behavior is a sure-fire way to get the youngest and the oldest pulling up their own socks to stuff themselves back into the spotlight again.

The Youngest

Ah yes, the baby of the family. Often the intended target of the "It's not fair" argument and commonly regarded as the favorite. Particularly by the sibling next up the line, whose once-secure role has been usurped by this snot-nosed pretender to the golden-child throne. What's interesting with this position is that often the older siblings discount them, and their abilities, allowing for any small achievement to be heralded as miraculous by the parents. Older siblings often tend to think of their younger siblings as incapable of doing the simplest of tasks, so impressing them is easy as well. Want to encourage older siblings to take on more responsibility? Try giving the baby a chore (like mowing the lawn) a few years earlier than their brothers and sisters were "allowed" to do it. Let the games begin.

The Only Child

The Prince. The Princess. The apple of the over-protective parental eye (it's a tough job, protecting an "only" prodigy from the big, bad world). Parents of one child will adamantly state that there is no truth to the only-child syndrome, but parents of more than one child know what a different parent they are when only one of those children is around. More patience, more indulgence, more bonding time. Good or bad, one child gets all the focus. But just like with a company that has only has one product, it's risky business putting all your fertilized eggs into one basket. It might be good to consider training a show dog (an actual canine) that you can fall back on should this prototype child not come up to industry standard.

The Teenager

Yes, teenagers can and do fit into all of the above categories, but wouldn't you agree that they are often in a category all of their own? Author Judith Martin summed it up nicely in *Miss Manners' Guide for the Turn-of-the-Millennium* when she called the invention of the teenager "a mistake." She argues that once you assign a name to a time in one's life when you don't have to pay taxes and get to stay out as late as you want, no one will want to live any differently.

While Ms. Martin has defined the teenage years to a T, would we really want to go back to being a teenager? Besides the sleeping and tax benefits, it's riddled with challenges. It's a time in one's life that's filled with angst, self-confidence issues, body issues, stress, and important life decisions. But mostly we wouldn't want to go back because thinking you know everything when you actually know very little is, well, embarrassing.

On a certain level, I admire teenagers. They speak their mind, try new things, sleep away stress, and call bullshit when it's bullshit. And even when it's not. But being the parent of a teenager is not easy.

While we all know that deep down teenagers are seeking approval from their parents, this is in a huge conflict with their desire to not conform to their parents' way of thinking. Deploying reverse psychology on a two-year-old is easy ("No, you're not allowed to finish that milk before bedtime."), but using it on a teenager takes a little more finesse. They want to borrow the car? Of course . . . if the first ten times they do, they drop their little brother off at hockey practice, or pick Mom up from her "book club."[37] Acknowledging their new levels of

....

[37] Really? You know what I mean. Keep reading.

responsibility is key, but sometimes allowing them to have this responsibility loses its lustre when they think you approve.

I've read with interest the latest studies that suggest that more and more parents are allowing, perhaps even encouraging, their teenagers to have sex at home. We all know they're going to do it, so the argument goes, so why not have them do it at home where Mom and Dad can have a drawer full of condoms waiting? Oh wait, before I go on, a note to my own kids:

YES, THIS IS THE ONE AND ONLY SEX PORTION OF THE BOOK. SKIP TO THE NEXT STEP NOW OR TELL ME HOW MUCH I NEED TO TOP UP THE THERAPY FUND.

Sorry about that.

Most of the "experts" weighing in on the sex-at-home debate are parents who boldly suggest that they will be progressive and allow their children to have sex in their home (which is funny, since most parents never have sex at home). My first thought was, well, you just don't know where you'll come down on the issue until you actually have a teenager in your house. It's like trying to imagine life with a newborn before you've had a baby. Totally impossible, idealized, and ridiculous. "Yes, here you go, Johnny, here's a condom. Make sure your girlfriend is satisfied before you take care of yourself." Eww, right?

But then I realized there was a certain genius to taking this stance. What teenager ever wanted to do something (or someone, as the case may be) that his parents were *allowing* him to do? I'm not saying the act loses all of its appeal, but it does lose most, knowing that Mom and Dad are in the house while you're trying to, well, you know. Never being one to not take advantage of a good thing (nor, apparently, a double negative), I decided there are a few more things we should give our teenagers "permission" to actually do. Consider adding these directives to your own personal employee handbook:

- Smirking and eye-rolling are Pediatric Association–approved methods of stretching facial muscles and improving connectivity to the part of the brain that controls trigonometry. Carry on!

- Girls should wear their pants snugly around the lower part of their hips, as this will help the hips widen and make eventual childbirth easier. Boys who routinely wear pants around their knees have been scientifically proven to marry a woman "just like Mom" and to suffer hair loss. Scientists are puzzled by this. Don't question science, kids.

- Don't speak with clarity and respect. Grunting with an air of condescension and annoyance can actually soothe the vocal chords and allow for a continuation of one's tenure in the church choir.

- Get at least eight hours of screen time per day. Continued exposure to alternative methods of entertainment, such as street hockey, swimming, cycling, and running, can result in unsightly muscles and toned legs, and take away from the challenge of piercing a particularly thick area in the midsection.

- Pierce everything you can. Allowing air to flow freely through various body parts can improve circulation and clear the brain, allowing for early morning cheerfulness and conversation.
- Sleep only during daylight hours. Prolonged exposure to sunlight makes you more attractive to the opposite sex . . . who will just get in the way of fitting in your eight hours of screen time.
- Stay away from household chores. Pitching in to help your parents will only lead to favoritism and potential monetary rewards. Grunt at them about this if you have to.

Once they have permission, these acts will suffer from omission, in my experience.

So, are you feeling better acquainted with your staff? Do you have a more highly developed sense of control? That's great, but people management is just one thing you'll have to work through when it comes to being the boss. There are a ton of details to manage in a corporate environment. Prepare yourself for the ones you need to work through at home as well.

REAL-LIFE LESSON

Titles are important. And they are a cheap way to reward employees. When I worked at packaged-goods company Reckitt & Colman, I had a linguistically challenged job title that required me to say "Worcestershire sauce" on a regular basis. When you are the Assistant Product Manager of the aforementioned product, you do it a lot. And you get corrected a lot. Apparently, every-freaking-body in the world has a different way of pronouncing this word, and they all think you're an idiot when you don't say it the way they do. I learned that if you ever find yourself in a position where you can make up your own title, you should. I'm working on one now that will include the words *president* or *chief idea officer*. This tactic also works when motivating your children to do what you want them to do (and you'll laugh yourself silly when you hear what they come up with!).

CONTROL THE CHAOS

Sweating the Details Without Losing Your Mind

So here you are, feeling all accomplished because you've organized the hell out of your own little team. You've got a reporting-structure flow chart, job descriptions, a performance review schedule . . . the works. You are all over this being the boss thing. You are running a tight ship. You are in control.

You think so, huh? I hate to burst your happy little bubble, but have you given any thought to what you're going to do the first time a spat breaks out at the water cooler (or fridge)? Or how you'll handle it when a senior employee (or middle manager) shows up wearing an entirely inappropriate outfit (and, yes, Dad, Crocs count as inappropriate)? Have you laid out a plan for office etiquette, sick days, or complaints? No? Clearly, you've still got some work to do.

In the corporate world, effective bosses are effective partially because they've learned how to handle the details. They know how to manage the small things and not let the small things manage them. A meeting ran too long or the seventh-floor coffee pot is broken? We can take care of that without blowing up the whole organization. You can do the same thing at home. The best place to start? Knowing what that "small stuff" is.

"IT'S NOT FAIR": MANAGING COMPLAINTS

Complaints are, hands down, the number one thing that a human resources department has to deal with. Coincidentally, complaints are also the number one thing parents have to deal with. While complaints in the kitchen or playroom manifest themselves differently than they do in the office, there are some startling similarities.

Breakdown of Complaints: Office and Home

EMPLOYEES	CHILDREN
Register formal complaints about performance review disagreements.	"It's not fair!"
Snipe and gossip at the water cooler about that bitch who just got promoted.	"It's not fair!"
Complain that their work assignments are beneath their level of expertise.	"It's not fair!"
Make fun of latest company slogan or "call to sales."[38]	"It's stupid!"

....

[38] Totally warranted in most cases, FYI.

On the other side of the coin, many of the complaints made by children also have a corporate response.

Breakdown of Complaints: Home and Office

CHILDREN	EMPLOYEE
"I shouldn't have to clean up my room if he doesn't have to."	Employee favoritism: "I organized the last Diversity Day!"
"This dinner sucks."	Employee complaint: "Why is the coffee on our floor so bad?"
"I didn't break it on purpose."	Team effort: "Pretty sure that was marketing's fault."

As we've already discussed, one of the tenets of human resources is to make sure that all employees are treated in a fair, respectful, and professional manner. The tenets of being a mother include: ensuring that all children are given the perception that they are being treated fairly, teaching respectful behavior (or at least calming down the swearing in public), and establishing some manners (or at least discouraging farting at the bus stop). No matter how much effort Mom puts in on these fronts, it will not stop children from declaring that someone else is indeed the favorite or from screeching, "It's not fair" on a fairly regular basis. (Nor will it prevent a mother from having a favorite child, upon occasion, and in a rotating fashion.)

So we've established – clearly – that complaints are going to happen. The question becomes, then, how to deal with them. Use this convenient form and get it in (quiet) writing or, depending on the employee's age, drawing. This is a lovely replacement for their actual voices.

STANDARD-ISSUE COMPLAINT FORM FOR JUNIOR EMPLOYEES

Name: _____

Age at time of complaint:* _____

*No, I can't see those fingers you're holding up. Seriously, if you're that young, you have nothing to complain about. Go throw this in the garbage. Now.

Nature of complaint (please check all that apply):**

_____ Sibling annoyance   _____ Meal concern†   _____ Funding

_____ Drive to mall   _____ Car accessibility _____ Rules

_____ Dress code   _____ Curfew   _____ Makeup

_____ Dad's jokes   _____ Mom's outfit   _____ Chores

_____ Family gatherings

**Please note that any complaints that fall into the "It's not fair" category will be summarily dismissed under the "No one ever said life was fair" statute of 1885.
†If Mom cooked the meal, she doesn't care. Eat this paper if you're so unhappy.

Please describe the complaint in 100 words or less. Note that terms such as *idiot, disgusting, loser,* and *suck* will be struck and rendered meaningless.

_____

_____

_____

For office use only:

Resolution suggested:

_____ Extended summer camp for offender

_____ Allowance disruption/reduction

_____ Grounding

_____ Grounding with electronics allowed

_____ No electronics

_____ Being forced to watch *Glee*

_____ Being forced to miss *Glee*

I'm not saying you should never listen to your children.[39] Go ahead and listen. Then make a decision on how to resolve the complaint, or don't. They may just have to, in the wise old words of my parents' generation, "suck it up." And then (and here's the really important part) *stick to your decision*. Kids can smell uncertainty a mile away. Give them an inch and you'll be giving them another twenty dollars. It's important for children to know that you are listening to them, and that they have been heard, even if it doesn't alter how you've chosen to deal with the complaint. Because you know one day they're going to say, "You don't remember me telling you that, do you?" and you want to be able to counter it with the advice you gave the first time.[40]

....

[39] Not really. Just most of the time.

[40] And if you can't remember, you can fake it. Trust me.

PARKING PASSES

You might think that a lot of the smaller details a manager in an office has to deal with won't apply at home. Wrong. But the good news is that there are policies in place in an office that we can steal for our own evil purposes on the home front. For example, how would the concept of a parking pass be translated to life at home?

If you're a regular sort of family, like mine, your garage is full of wheeled vehicles, such as bikes, trikes, skateboards, scooters, wagons, strollers, and doll prams. Give your kids the option to "own and store" no more than eight wheels at a time (wagon/scooter, scooter/bike/skateboard) and get rid of some of that clutter.

CUBICLE ASSIGNMENTS

Nothing induces more infighting than the assignment of choice cubicles at the office. Where you *do* sit is just as important as where you *don't* sit. Against the window? Nice. Next to the administrative assistant? Get that résumé ready. With a utility pole in the middle of your workspace? Clearly you need to suck up more. Oh, those human resources people know exactly what they're doing when they "arbitrarily" reduce cubicle space; don't kid yourself. At one of the offices I worked in, people would put in overtime just so they could move walls and have a bigger cubicle than their now-squished neighbor.

In the typical North American home, walls are somewhat more permanent than cubicle dividers. While this might solve the territory encroachment problem, it doesn't mean you won't have territory wars over who gets which room or who shares with whom. If you have ever seriously considered giving your child(ren) the master bedroom, please stop reading this book now. I can't help you.

For the rest of you, there are some basic criteria to keep in mind when assigning bedrooms in the house. Infants probably belong in the room closest to you. This is as much about being able to hear them should they wake up in the middle of the night as it is about you stumbling down the hall in the dark at 2:00 a.m. and doing minimal damage to your toes and shins as you bang along your no-doubt cluttered hallway. (You have a newborn, right? This is normal.) As the kids get older, you want to move them farther and farther away from you. It's okay to tell your eight-year-old: "I don't care if you're having a nightmare, me coming into your room is going to be scarier than that, let me tell you." You can easily yell this across a landing, BTW. And if they respond by turning on their light and firing up their Nintendo DS, well, hopefully you can't hear it from your room. As the kids develop into teenagers and acquire (ugh) social lives of their own, you will quickly discover that you are indeed "old enough" to have a teenager. This is evidenced by the fact that you go to bed hours before they come in. And their curfew is 11:00 p.m. When teenage boys come home, whatever activity they have been engaged in beforehand will have necessitated a three-thousand-calorie top-up, at least. This will involve the slamming of the fridge door, the beeping of the microwave, and the crashing of plates (on the counter, not in the dishwasher – don't be crazy). If you can manage it, a kitchen door that actually closes is ideal. You also want his room located as far away from yours as possible. A lower level is ideal. This will also prepare you for when he makes the "big move" out of the house and away to some sort of post-secondary education facility. Not only can't you hear what he's doing, but you'll discover that you don't really care; you're just so happy to be in bed at 9:30 p.m. without fear of being woken.

When your college-aged children come back home for the holidays, try to have a business case ready for why they should sleep in the basement. It's 100 percent certain that they will at some point say, "When I'm living in residence you have no idea what time I get home. I'm coming home at 3:00 a.m. here too." They will not believe you when you say that it's not about trust, it's just that you don't want to be woken up. Be prepared.

Assign rooms wisely, and well. And if they have a problem with it? That's right . . . you're the boss!

SICK DAYS

One of the nice things about having a "real" job outside the home is that you have the ability,[41] nay, perhaps the obligation, to call in sick once in a while. Employers can be funny with the concept of sick days. They will swear that they don't want you coming in and infecting the whole office, yet with every sick call received there is an element of skepticism whether the illness is, in fact, severe enough to stop you from coming in and fulfilling your duties as Accounts Receivable Clerk, Mustard Products. Clearly a position like this cannot be left untended for even one day.

Sick days in the business of being a family have slightly larger repercussions than the mustard invoicing going undone. If a child is sick, parents must scramble to get their ammunition together in terms of who has to sacrifice more (workwise) to take care of said child. My advice to moms who work outside the home? Always be prepared with a fail-safe list of work-related items with which to counter-pitch your husband. This list could include such items as "all day off-site to determine bonus structure" or the unbeatable "command-performance town hall." Once it has been established that child care can take place, calls to school, karate studios, hockey coaches, and the like must commence. Your child does not live in a vacuum – there

....

[41] *Real* for most people is defined by the fact that there is an awful commute with awful people involved, and your workspace resembles an awful veal-fattening pen.

are many, many people who need to know of her illness. If you do find yourself in the unfortunate position where you and your spouse simply cannot care for the child without a serious effect on your work or social life (do you know how hard it is to book that eyebrow woman?), you must start in on the network of in-laws, friends who owe favors, and paid babysitters who have gotten over the last unfortunate strawberry-jam-in-the-DVD-player episode. It is interesting to note that you will instantly know when all of your arrangements are secured: the exact moment said 'sick' child will be seen skipping through the house and taunting her siblings with the "I'm too sick to go to school and you aren't" chant, with nary a sign of the illness that had plagued her so severely. At this point, however, it's too late and too complicated to untangle all of the child-care arrangements, so as far as you're concerned, she's still sick.

If I look back on all the times I, as a child, attempted to fake sick for my own mom, I'm actually embarrassed. It's so ridiculously easy to tell when a child is faking! Stomach ache? Tell them to go poo. Headache? Announce that you're taking them in for a brain scan. Remind them that if they miss school for the scan, they miss any extracurricular activities too (mention only the ones they actually like. In fact, why are they enrolled in some they don't?) and that there is a "sick-kid-bedtime" policy as well. Make it the same time their favorite show comes on or at least a half-hour earlier than their next-youngest sibling.

In a work environment, there are a set number of sick days assigned to each employee, and each of these is logged as it occurs. This is a good idea at home too. Put a note in your employee's personnel (or personal) file every time a sick day occurs. The inconvenience caused for Mom and Dad when it comes to covering these days could be detrimental to their future promotability and compensation.

Now, when it comes to Mom or Dad waking up under the weather, two totally different outcomes occur. When Dad is ill, it will be with the dreaded "man-flu," which apparently is worse than all of your PMS, childbirth, and mastitis pain put together.[42] He will render himself totally unable to do the simplest of tasks – fixing anything to eat or drink, showering, shaving . . . it all goes out the window. He will have a tremendous ability to nap. The best is when he tries to pretend to put on a brave face: "Oh really. It's nothing" *Cough. Cough.* Damn right it's nothing. Have a baby and then call me.

When Mom is sick, on the other hand, she goes to work and/or continues carrying on with running the household. Most often, the discovery of Mom's illness will come only after the sound of squealing tires from Dad's car can be heard. Dads are great at spotting an under-the-weather wife and getting the hell out of Dodge in their own Dodge, thereby dodging any domestic duty.

....

[42] Not really.

Husbands deny their wives are really sick when they have a game to get to with the same fervor that moms deny their child is sick when they have a girls' getaway planned.[43]

In the interest of keeping family peace (and sanity), here are some easy-to-follow guidelines to tell if a member of your family is really sick or faking.

- **How to tell if a child is really sick:** Fortunately, most children are very bad actors/liars. You know they're faking their illness if they: a) have a test at school that day, b) clutch their stomach seconds after bounding down the stairs and punching a brother on the way, c) are hovering suspiciously near a heating vent with a thermometer, or d) ask, "What happens if I feel better around four?" noting a hockey game on the schedule for later that day. A gentle reminder about their allotted number of sick days and the impact on their compensation or negotiating position when it comes to extended curfews and chances of borrowing the car is recommended.
- **How to tell if a husband is really sick:** Guys can be tricky. Some are entirely stoic about broken bones, huge bleeding wounds, and things that went *snap*, but the slightest sniffle can have them heading for the nearest couch wrapped in a Snuggie. My teenage son broke a collarbone at camp one year and didn't complain about it until about a week later,

---

[43] The girls' weekend, by the way, is an urban myth. One has never been known to ever get past the "we should have a girls' getaway" verbal planning stage.

when it was "bugging" him. This is the same kid who used to writhe in pain for three days after having his braces tightened. The "man-flu" is well documented and needs no additional space here; we've all had the flu, it sucks, get over yourself. You don't need to announce every little symptom and sigh every ten minutes. Bottom line? Who cares if he's sick? He's an adult. Let him figure it out.

- **How to tell if a wife is really sick**: Because she says so.

A final note to moms on the topic of sick days: I know of lots of women who complain that when they are sick, they're expected to soldier on with all their responsibilities, but when their husbands are sick, they "get to" lie in bed all day and milk it. This perplexes me. If you want to lie in bed all day when you're sick, do it. If they can get away with it, so can you. If we force ourselves to carry on (which I'm not entirely opposed to in a mind-over-matter sort of a way), it's a bit ridiculous to then feel resentful of someone handling a situation in a way that we say we wish we could but don't. Aren't you the boss of yourself too?

I often joke that in my next life I want to come back as a man. Or at least live like one. You women might know what I mean. Men just don't have as highly developed a guilt gene as we do. This allows them to sit on the couch while children spill things, read the paper while brothers punch, and go to the grocery store and only buy what's on the list. The list their wives made for them. It's a very black-and-white world in which they live. If they invite people over, they just invite whomever they happen to be thinking about at the time. They don't deliberately *not* invite certain people over . . . or only invite people just to annoy others . . . not that I would ever do that.[44] Do you see what I mean about them being simpler?

The same comes to sick days. When they're sick, they stay in bed and expect the world to carry on just fine without them. And it usually does. When we're sick, we either bark commands from our bed or trudge through the house/office getting things done because if we don't, no one else will. Which, of course, is garbage. Next time you're sick, just think to yourself, what would my husband do? Then roll over and close your eyes.

OFFICE ETIQUETTE

Once upon a time, my then seven-year-old son received a school award for "Courtesy and Kind Cooperation," handed out in a morning assembly. Later that afternoon, as he sat on the floor of the grocery store screaming because I wouldn't buy him some fruit gummies, I asked Mr. Freakin' Courtesy why he acted like this with me but obviously not with his teacher. "Because I know you better," he replied. Right. The old familiarity-breeds-contempt rule again. (Well, I was certainly contemptuous of his familiarity with a meltdown.)

....

[44] This week.

At first glance, the office hardly seems like a place to look to for guidance when it comes to manners and decorum. As workplaces (and workplace relationships) have gotten more casual, workplace manners and etiquette have definitely hit the skids. The doofus from human resources (who should know better, by the way) comes down to the second floor and steals the last cup of coffee. Not only does he fail to start the new pot, he leaves the glass carafe on the burner to crack – only after it has spewed burnt coffee scent throughout the entire office. Sound familiar?

I remember working at a large soft-drink manufacturing company in the early 1980s. We called the president Mr. Smith.[45] He had a big corner office, an administrative assistant stationed out front, and an imposing manner positioned inside. No one questioned him about where his coffee came from, or even looked him in the eye. No one questioned why he had to have the staples on all documents placed on the diagonal, exactly an inch and a half from the outside edge of the paper. Or why he was led away by men in blue suits one day, never to return. But I digress. I wonder how my kids would take to calling me Ms. Buckworth? It certainly seemed to work in terms of structure and getting things done in that office.

Given that this type of formality seems like a long shot, parents have to come up with other ways to raise the bar when it

....

[45] Name changed to protect the inappropriate.

comes to basic manners. Instead of thinking of the way employees treat each other (and being horrified with the results),
why not consider the way in which you, as a boss, might
instruct your employees to deal with the general public?

I have a friend whose daughter consistently calls me
"dude." Not only am I not a dude,[46] but I think this type of
language implies a sense of familiarity we just don't have.
I have not corrected her, but if my children were to do the
same thing, I would do so quickly. Listen to the way your
children speak to other adults and correct them. They are not
their equals, and they shouldn't be allowed to treat them that
way. Children are not "little adults." They're children. And
they should never, ever call their mother by her first name.

The same type of thing occurs in supposedly fine restaurants. Say you're there with a group of your female friends.
You sit down and wait for the server to approach. He arrives,
smiles, and says, "Can I get you guys anything to drink?"
Not a fan. There's such a disconnection between the language that's being used and the environment in which it's
being used. The same could be true with a receptionist
greeting an office visitor with "'Sup?" or a junior sales
representative telling his potential customer how he's been
with the wrong supplier all these years.

Since we are at our most casual (and non-cooperative,
apparently) at home, our language and manners are most

....

[46] Last time I checked.

likely to slip there. Yet, paradoxically, this is where we learn most of them as well.

So what's a parent to do? At our house, we've always treated Sunday dinner as a bit of a social experiment. We sit at the dining room table (versus the kitchen table), and the kids are expected to place their cloth napkins on their laps and use their utensils appropriately. Just for an extra touch, we play classical music. While the kids squirm and complain about the setting and the sounds, I try to convince myself that our perseverance in teaching them good table and social manners will pay off. And it has.

My oldest daughter, away at university and out for dinner with her boyfriend at a nice restaurant, took the time to BBM me this message:[47] "Out for dinner with B. Made him put his napkin on his lap. See what you've done to me? Thanks a lot."

Oh, I know she didn't really mean "thank you," but you know what I was thinking? "My work here is done."

Aside from Sunday dinner, what else can you do to foster good manners and etiquette at home?

Practice Restraint

Manners are something that we don't focus on in the workplace, but they exist, nonetheless, in our tone, demeanor, and ability not to throw a stapler at someone's head in a meeting when they're really pissing us off . . . that sort of

---

[47] Yes, I am aware that BBMing during dinner constitutes bad manners, but I'm making a point. Bear with me, okay?

thing. Some of this restraint would be well suited for our home lives as well, if we could transplant it. We don't have to say everything that comes into our heads, for instance (we can tweet it instead). Children aren't the only offenders here. Wives have long been guilty of saying such things to their husbands and children as:

"You're kidding me with that shirt, right?"

"Oh, did you want to be a part of this family?"

"So your football game is more important than your daughter's ballet class?"

None of these questions actually require asking, and I'll tell you why – everyone already knows the answers. They're not rhetorical questions exactly – rhetorical questions tend to have a passive answer. These are more like inflammatory questions, designed to get a rise out of the recipient.

Imagine, at work, if we were to say:

"You're kidding me with that project proposal, right?"

"Oh, so you decided not to be a team player like we had hoped."

"So you're telling me your daughter's ballet class is more important than this late-night budget meeting?"

Or:

"You know casual day is only on Friday, right? It's not Friday."

Pause.

"And even, then, there are rules. Perhaps you didn't get that memo."

Children in particular have a hard time with restraint. Acting on natural impulses is, well, just a natural impulse to them. But it's important to make sure you instill in them the philosophy of being able to *think* whatever they want but to use a strong filter when it comes to the words coming out of their mouths. This is particularly true during the teenage years. For example:

WRONG APPROACH: Teenage Daughter: "Are you wearing that outside the house, Mom? Just asking."
RIGHT APPROACH: Teenage Daughter: (silence)
WRONG APPROACH: Teenage Son: "Cool story, Mom, tell it again. Only this time make it interesting."
RIGHT APPROACH: Teenage Son: "Huh."

Reinforce with your kids that the less we know what they're thinking (by what's coming out of their mouths), the more likely they are to be able to borrow the car.

Act as If

Building family morale is tricky. It can be hard to get every member of your family to feel happy at the same time. Sometimes just seeing a sibling look happy is enough to make another sibling unhappy. And, at a certain time of the month, just seeing your husband *not* be miserable (like you are) can be bad for morale.

But can't we all just pretend to be playing Happy Family? Maybe not all the time, but there is something to the "fake it till you make it" philosophy of at least pretending that things are going well, particularly when you're handling

things around your children. I think the very seeds of polite-
ness come from masking our true feelings and trying to
make sure everyone is "okay." And I am "okay" with this.
There's no need to make children aware of every bad thing
that is going on in your life, but sometimes it's a good thing
to let them know if you are facing particular challenges,
both at work and at home, so that they can appreciate why
Mom is a little snippy at the dinner table or why Dad is not
interested in playing a marathon session of Monopoly.

I'm not saying you have to go around looking like grin-
ning idiots all the time and bursting into a chorus of "Put on
a Happy Face" every ten minutes. And try not to look overly
excited when you get confirmation of an extended business
trip. We know it's good; but they don't need to know that.

Good etiquette can and should come in the form of trying to
make people feel good or, at a minimum, not feel bad. In the
business world, we like to call this being "politically correct."

At work:

Boss: I think your latest status report is a little short on
   details.[48] However, the creative spelling license you
   took is to be commended, if not repeated.[49]
Employee: Gee, thanks, boss!

....

[48] You spent five minutes on this and it shows. You're incompetent.
[49] Learn how to spell, doofus.

At home:

Mom/Boss: I think your English essay is a little short. And while I admire your creativity in using that particular font size, I'm not sure that's what the teacher meant when she said, "Fill five pages."

Child: I think it's fine.

Mom/Boss: Fine. I'm not the boss of you at school, so good luck with that.

Bottom line? Manners count. When trying to instill a basic sense of decency in your children, it may help to remember that long explanations are not needed. "That's bad manners" is enough.

INTEROFFICE RELATIONSHIPS: SIBLING RIVALRY

Have you ever worked in an office where people didn't get along? Er . . . have you ever worked in an office? It's funny how the big things (utter and complete incompetency, for instance) will slide right on by, like water off a duck's back, while the little things (failure to wipe coffee drips off the kitchen counter) can drive you to distraction. This truism is magnified about a thousandfold at home. Consider the sibling who pokes his brother fourteen times with a stick until he finally retaliates with a whack upside the head. Or the one who says, "What? What? What?" over and over again as her sister attempts to report a farting incident. Bear in mind that siblings spend somewhere in the range of eight hours a day together, occasionally more. And most of those hours are rife with potential disaster as they occur a) in the early morning, when the combination of stunned brother and sarcastic sister is at its worst, or b) in the evening during Family Squabble Time (i.e., dinner) or the homework hours, chased by the ritual fighting over the television remote and topped off by the always popular "who has to go to bed first" debate. These trivial incidents make up most of childhood, and, yes, the importance of whether your brother called you a spaz or not takes on great significance in these trying conditions.

As the boss of your own dysfunctional family unit, it falls to you to sort out the interoffice relationships. Clearly, you're going to want to keep fighting to a minimum, or at least to a dull roar. Think twice, though, before you try to eradicate it altogether. As a manager, I learned there's almost nothing more fun or rewarding than having two employees who don't get along. No, really. When this happens in the office, there is increased competition (i.e., output), shared information (i.e., gossip about that other employee), and a confidence or bonding that takes place as they assume some sort of empathy with you, their "fair" manager. The thing is, you have to side with both of them or face the wrath of the human resource tribunal. Trust me; you don't want to go there. The same applies with your children when they fight. The key difference? Fights in the office environment have to stay within certain boundaries (so say the labor laws), whereas at home the gloves are usually off. Siblings are not generally punished in any significant way for slagging off their co-worker/brother; oftentimes, in fact, teasing is something that we suggest they learn how to take once in a while.

But how do you know when the line separating good old-fashioned rivalry and true bullying has been crossed? And when should you, the boss, step in and shut down what might have become a one-way barrage of insults or jibes? The same rules apply both at the office and at home.

Five Tips for Encouraging Healthy Interfamily Relationships

1) Remarks about personal appearance are never allowed – particularly regarding things that cannot be changed (size of nose, height, birthmarks, etc.).

2) Questions regarding parentage – or speculations as to the nature of said parents – are discouraged.

3) Any sort of physical touching, pushing, poking, pinching, smacking, slapping, tripping, kicking, shoving, whacking, snapping, flicking, picking, or bopping is frowned upon, even if it occurs "by accident."[50]

4) No food throwing. Ever.

5) They are not the boss of each other. You are the boss of them. Ergo, they can't boss each other around. Put a stop to it, early and often.

....

[50] We're on to you. That wasn't an accident. Nice try.

Finally, should any employee or child begin a discussion with "It's not fair," you have the full authority to make it so. That'll teach 'em.

CASUAL DAY

Back when I was the boss in an actual office, I was not pleased when this thing called Casual Day came around. In fact, I was mortified. Wasn't it enough to watch my husband slouch around in his fleece and mom jeans at home? Now I had to watch other guys do it too? And do you know what's worse than seeing a female co-worker look absolutely horrible in her skin-tight blue jeans? Seeing a female colleague look absolutely smokin' in them.

When I worked for CIBC, a Casual Friday policy was introduced to the company. And of course this was an official "policy." I can't even imagine the number of person-hours that must have been spent constructing this policy, which came to include such qualifiers as no tube tops,[51] T-shirts with inappropriate messages, or flip-flops. Basically everything else was allowed. Which left the door wide open to badly fitting jeans (too high-waisted or, worse, too low), tank tops, sweatpants, and (shudder) fleece. Most of the men in the bank took to wearing one of two outfits: the

....

[51] The fact that we have to tell gainfully employed people this disturbs me.

corporate Casual Guy wardrobe of beige pleated khakis and a faux denim shirt, or a golf shirt with ironed jeans. If they can find a way to work corporate logos into these two ensembles, oh believe me, they will.

The women tended to go the other way a bit – the younger women would bring out their clubbing gear and the older ones would raid Tabi during their two-for-one sales.[52] What I'm trying to get across here is that it wasn't a good thing. A well-fitted suit, or even just a blazer, can hide a multitude of sins (e.g., chardonnay consumption).

And so I rebelled by continuing to wear suits, skirts, and blazers on Fridays. I had many sins to cover up (a few pregnancies, remember?). Apparently this made me uptight. But it also made me feel like I wasn't the mailroom clerk. Which I wasn't. Not that there is anything wrong with being a mailroom clerk if that's where you want to be. But I didn't want to be in the mailroom; I wanted to be in the corner office. So I dressed for where I wanted to go instead of where I had already come from.

My husband e-mailed me from his office one day to announce that the world was coming to an end: someone had passed him in the hallway wearing Crocs. Even though they were black Crocs, I advised him to fire the offender. Immediately.

While we can't fire our children (I keep trying) for wearing Crocs or other ridiculous and offensive clothing items, we can

---

[52] Which I believe is an acronym for Too Ample Butts, Inc.

throw out those items when they're not looking. Letting the clothing go seems preferable to turfing the kid, no?

Instill in your children a sense of looking good and feeling good when they are young and it will stay with them. Tell them it's a sign of respect for the people around them. There's a lot to be said for leading by example on this front.

Saturday Night Live once did a hysterical ad for mom jeans, in which the tagline was, "Because I'm not a woman. I'm a mom." Sadly, I don't think all moms got the memo that this was intended to be a joke. It comes down to this: if you are leaving the house, please dress as though you are leaving the house. Thanks.

Okay, okay. Settle down. While I agree in principle that who you really are inside, and what you're capable of, is way more important than how you look on the outside, you may not get the chance to prove what you're made of if you're labeled immediately as something else (i.e., a slob).

I hear some moms actually complain about the lipstick-and-heels moms they see in the school yard. They think they are pretentious or showing off. Mostly I think the sweatpants moms feel a tad inferior and/or lazy when they haven't made an effort and maybe could have. Do we really need to tear other women down for feeling good about how they look? I'm working on that playground dress code now. In the meantime, here are some tips on how to get your family sorted out so they don't embarrass you in public.

Five Rules for Dressing the Family

1) Matching outfits: Should be avoided at all costs unless you are taking a photo for an ironic Christmas card, in bad matching holiday sweaters. Then, totally allowable. Although somewhat "done."

2) No orange sweatpants. Ever. (You know who you are.)

3) Allowing your children to wear their ballet outfits/ soccer clothes/hockey shorts anywhere other than on the trips to and from the arena, and maybe the occasional pit stop at a coffee shop, is strictly forbidden. You don't need to prove to the world your children participate in these very worthwhile activities. We get it.

4) Pajama pants. Never never never. If you let them wear these out of the house when they're three, they'll be doing it when they're thirteen. Body parts that don't move when a child is three somehow manage to juggle and jiggle and stick out when they're thirteen.

5) Socks and sandals. Yes, it needed its own point.

The devil is certainly in the details, or if not the devil, at least the potential death of your sanity. But once you've mastered these details, your life should be immeasurably easier. Unfortunately, not all "details" are human (a species, after all, that can generally be negotiated with). Some details involve paperwork. Mounds and mounds of paperwork. Brace yourself for some nasty paper cuts because that's where we're headed next.

REAL-LIFE LESSON

My last full-time corporate position was as director of marketing for the co-branded credit card portfolio at CIBC. The job included negotiating and working with such companies as Air Canada, The Bay, Shoppers Drug Mart, and others. The most valuable lesson I learned when in the throes of contract negotiation with these organizations was that no matter how small a detail might seem, getting it down on paper, in the contract, was key in moving the relationship forward in a clear and concise manner. Ever had one of those conversations with your kids or husband where you wish you had a piece of paper to whip out and wave in their face? Make a habit of writing things now, and next time, you will!

GET ORGANIZED

Winning the Paper Chase

Thirty years ago when we thought we'd all be driving flying cars and getting down the street on moving sidewalks, we also had this science-fiction fantasy that we'd live in a paperless world. Look around your office and home right now. Look paperless to you? Didn't think so. From printed PowerPoint decks to contracts to day-care release forms to lunch-monitor rules, paper is still prevalent and still necessary when it comes to keeping things running smoothly. Somehow, dealing with details on paper is a lot easier than sliding them across a touchscreen.

So slip on your paper-cut-protector thimble and wade in.

MONEY, MONEY, MONEY

Although it's true that less and less money is actually paper these days – not to mention bills, which come electronically in many households – dealing with money issues is probably the single most important way in which a boss can get herself organized. From negotiating allowances (also known as mostly unearned salaries) to justifying the purchase of that $140 swimsuit (that will never see the light of day but looked fabulous in that skinny-mirrored, dimly lit change room), balancing the family books is not an activity for the faint of heart. Money doesn't grow on trees. In fact, when you have a family of six, it falls through your pockets faster than the curve of your butt on your fortieth birthday.

It goes without saying – but you know me, I'll say it anyway – that children are the biggest challenge when it comes to conquering the family budget. They may be cute,[53] but they're also expensive. Apparently, it costs about $200,000 to raise a child in North America – and this number excludes the therapy now required to get your head around that figure, and competitive-level sports fees. How exactly does this monstrous figure break down? Turn the page and let's find out.

....

[53] Though not all the time.

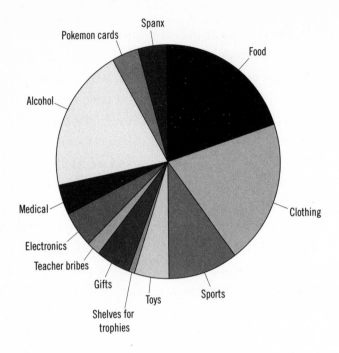

(Those of you who are questioning the "alcohol" and "Spanx" categories as a cost of having children clearly don't have any.[54])

There's no doubt about it – financial planning for families can be tough. You're always going to have competing priorities: the bathroom renovation or the summer holiday; the new hockey equipment or replacing the suddenly too-small bike. How's a mom to manage? It all starts with the budget.

....

[54] Also be warned that excessive use of either of these could contribute to having children, necessitating more of each. It's a vicious circle.

The Big, Bad Budget

Do you have a household budget? Imagine operating a successful business and not keeping track of the books. It wouldn't actually be a successful business for very long. Whether you're managing a GM-sized multinational, a one-person web-design business, or a family of four, it's essential to keep track of the money coming in and the money going out. In the business world, entire well-staffed (and generally humorless) departments spend their days running profit-and-loss statements, cost–benefit analyses, and budget after budget. Unless you happen to love this stuff – and, hey, there's no accounting (ha!) for taste – you don't need to get this complicated at home. Apply the KISS principle here and keep it simple. There are some terrific online programs that will connect your bank account to your bills paid to your income to your invoicing, and so on. If you're a process person, you'll want to look into that; if you're not, rest easy. Budgeting can be pretty low-tech. Enter . . . cue the drum roll . . . the spreadsheet.

FAMILY BUDGET	JAN	FEB	MAR	APR	MAY	JUN
Income:						
Mom						
Dad						
Total Income:						
Expected Tax Rate:						
Net (Real) Income:						
Expenses:						
Mortgage						
Car Payments						
Insurance						
Hydro						
Telephone/Internet						
Cell						
Cable						
Gas						
Transit						
Clothing						
Food						
Entertainment						
Household						
Totals:						

JUL	AUG	SEP	OCT	NOV	DEC	TOTAL

That's not too scary, is it? This is about as basic a budget as you can get.[55] Some people find it hard to wrap their heads around an annual budget, but breaking things down by month like this can really help. The spreadsheet makes it easy to see, at a glance, when the big expenses (Christmas, college tuition, car insurance for teenagers) will be coming down the pipe. If you're lucky, one or two of these times will correspond with an uptick in earnings (e.g., a year-end bonus, a tax return).

Of course all of us are going to have different expenses, and you may have one-time expenses that float in and out. Other categories might include sports registration fees, sports tournament fees, ridiculously overpriced sports equipment and the team track suits that go with them, orthodontist bills, therapy fund for the orthodontic work, therapy fund in general, pedicures, cute pillows for the living room, etc.

Of course there's always the challenge around "fixed" expenses that seem to always have special "add-on" charges, such as car maintenance, home repair, and wardrobe adjustment after a two-week holiday in Italy. Take my advice and marry someone handy. Too late? Join the club.

The key is to set up a basic budget that works for your family's particular needs. It can be as simple or as complex as you'd like it to be, but remember that the more detail you include, the clearer the financial picture will be.

....

[55] Or that I can think of.

Money Out: Fixed Expenses and Other Fun

If your family is like most families (and most companies, come to think of it), you'll likely find yourselves struggling to keep a list of the money flowing *out* of your house, while trying to maximize the money flowing *in*. And more power to you! The basis of a happy, healthy financial life is, after all, making sure that you don't run out of money before you run out of month. So how do you do this? You start by getting a grip on your family's fixed expenses. Fixed expenses are non-negotiables that must appear in your budget every single month – think mortgage/rent, groceries, electricity, etc. Stuff you can't live without. Let's take a look at a few of these fixed expenses in more detail.

Groceries

Whether it's with the healthy stuff (what the hell is quinoa, anyway?), the pre-packaged stuff, or the really-bad-for-you stuff, we need to keep our families fed and happy. Not necessarily at the same time. In fact, I've found this to be mostly impossible. Groceries can be a *huge* expense in a household with lots of children, particularly if some of them are of the teenage boy variety. If you're trying to tame expenses in this area without succumbing to an "all ramen noodles all the time" diet, consider:

- Shop only the outside aisles of the supermarket. This is where all the fresh produce, dairy, and meat can be found, along with end-of-aisle specials. The foods in these sections are the most cost-effective items you can buy. Prepared, pre-packaged foods cost more because (stay with me on this) they are prepared and packaged for you. Make a detour only for the coffee section.

- Don't bring children who are old enough to troll the aisles by themselves and come back loaded down with all kinds of junk food. You'll either have to deal with arguing in the aisles or just give in. And neither of these options is very boss like.

- Don't shop when you're hungry or suffering from the consequences of a night out with your colleagues (other mom bosses). You'll get home with fourteen different types of beverage, nachos, and a dozen chocolate croissants.[56]

- Try to shop at the same time as that sanctimonious health-freak mom on your street. You'll be too embarrassed to put the high-fat, high-cost foods into your cart. Won't you? What will that do to your family brand?

Clothing

When kids are young this is a no-brainer. Their addled brains are so full of intellectual thoughts such as "Why is Mommy's bum so big?" and "I wonder if I can eat that" to spend any time at all worrying about what they're wearing. *You* decide what they wear. It's almost like a company uniform. In fact . . . no . . . that would never work. Or would it? Yes! Forget the *school* uniform, let's look at a way to take all

....

[56] Or is that just me? Never mind. Just don't shop when you're hungry.

of the drama out of dressing our families and put them in the same outfits! Too much? I'm *so* going to work on this.

But getting back on track – when kids are young they want clothes that make them feel good. A beaming Bob the Builder, Barbie, or Hot Wheels shirt makes your child feel like he or she actually lives in that magical world (have I mentioned that children aren't really that bright?). The best part? Due to the transient nature of said child's interest in these characters, you can buy low-quality clothing from a deep-discounted store and not really care whether the item falls apart after the first wash. The purchasing challenges associated with clothing come more when the children are a little older and realize they want to trade in the bulldozer logo for the crocodile logo, or the eagle logo, or the big letter *H*, or whatever it is that they see the "cool kids" wearing. But they're still outgrowing clothes at the speed of light. You'll need to make good decisions about how and where to spend your tight clothing budget.

Speaking of tight . . . good luck to you if you are the parent of a teenage girl. Now you have to weigh another factor besides quality, coolness, and price – suitability. Again, maybe we should seriously consider a family uniform. It worked for the Von Trapps, didn't it? Note to self: put flowery drapes and a nautical whistle on the shopping list/purchase order.

But back to the budget. Consider adopting the following guidelines when it comes to efficiently and economically clothing your brood:

- There shall be no more than four pairs of shoes (that fit) per child.
- There shall always be more than one pair of "perfect jeans" per tween or teen in order to avoid late-night washings and total freak-outs. Build this cost into your budget.
- You shall always use your (better) judgment. They are not smart enough to make the call on purchasing a branded piece of clothing versus a piece from a discount store. Luckily, you are. Use that. Like a boss would. Think hand-me-down. Where possible, buy clothes for the oldest that you can pass down to the youngest. But once in a while, let the one who is second or third in line pick out clothes for the older sibling, just to make it fair.
- No more stuffed toys. Full stop. They are totally embargoed. I know these are actually toys and not clothing, but you could have purchased enough clothes to dress an entire village with what you've spent on those stuffies.[57]

Furniture

We need to sit on, stand on, sleep in, lean against, eat off of, put feet up onto, and generally try to distinguish ourselves from cave dwellers through smart furniture purchases. Here are some guidelines to help you not exceed your budget for this cost center:

- Nothing white. Full stop. Nothing that can't be sprayed

....

[57] Not to mention the American Girl dolls.

with industrial cleaner, or, in a pinch, hosed down. Trust me on this one.

- Avoid sharp corners on low-lying tables. It's a real drag to go to the hospital for those head wounds, and the kids don't like it much either.
- If you have something antique, vintage, or fragile, rent storage space and put it there. This does not include your Aunt Dorothy, BTW.
- Before you buy a piece of furniture, take your kids to the store and have them try it out. If they break it, don't take it home. Maybe keep the car running.
- Leather, leather, leather. The more industrial-strength, the better. If you can Windex it without ruining it, you win.

Recreational Equipment and Tools

How many of us have an entire basement and/or garage filled with all kinds of sporting equipment that has only been used once? Look in my garage and you'll find bikes, skateboards, roller blades, canoes, kayaks, inflatable floaty things, baseballs, footballs, soccer balls, tennis balls, tennis racquets, and squash racquets. Is Dad on a new fitness plan? Is Mom trying to fit into her new jeans? Are the kids on a post–X _Games_ fan high? Whatever your circumstance, the sports-equipment people see you coming.

- Sports-equipment salespeople are generally on commission. They'll try to get you to upgrade everything to the "elite-athlete" level, even if it's for your three-year-old and her little tike hockey team.

- You really, really don't need a specialty helmet for every single sport. There's no such thing as a "toboggan helmet," okay? Use the one you already bought for skiing lessons.
- Encourage your kids to take up the same sports as each other – they can either see how easily their sibling gives up the sport or enter the world of hand-me-down hockey pants if it all works out.
- Push the kids to the sports with low-cost equipment. Why do you think soccer is so popular? I can't explain hockey, sorry.

Mom's Fixed Expenses

Before we leave the topic of fixed expenses, let's take a moment to acknowledge the fact that not everyone will have the same sense of what is 100 percent necessary. I can start with myself here. My own fixed expenses include:

- pedicures, manicures, waxing, massages, wraps, and basically any relaxing spa procedure; having a pair of black pants that fit at all times;
- hair treatments of any kind;
- chardonnay. I'm not explaining this. (You're really having a hard time knowing when I'm kidding, aren't you?[58]); and
- the perfect pair of black heels.

....

[58] Not actually kidding.

Dad's fixed expenses, on the other hand, might include:

- gadgety, screwy metal and wood thingies from Home Depot;
- that extra cable package. Really, who watches ESPN Classic? Doesn't that belong on the History Channel? Who watches *that*?
- an extra shirt to buy after the wife says, "No. I don't think so," when you put that other shirt on to go out for dinner.

While Junior's fixed expenses are likely:

- candy, video games, candy, video games, new hockey puck, candy, video games, etc.
- paper trading cards featuring Japanese evolving monsters of some sort or another. And the case to carry them in. THEY'RE MADE OF PAPER. YOU CAN PRINT THEM AT HOME.
- Markers. Because you can never find them for homework when you need them. Never.

Discretionary Expenses

Most corporate budgets include certain expenses that are first on the chopping block if sales take a dramatic downturn or if the CEO is replaced and the new one decides to "sharpen the pencil."[59] Think things like the company jet, the company holiday party, multicolored sticky notes, or

....

[59] No, it's not a sexual harassment thing. Calm down.

mechanical pencils, depending on the depth of the cuts. At home, easily axed items could include:

- hockey equipment. If it gets too small and uncomfortable for them to wear, or breaks so it's not safe for them to play in, you get to make them quit playing and save on the hockey registration as well. Score! (Literally.);
- everything on Dad's fixed-expenses list; and
- mostly everything on Junior's list as well, except the things that keep him occupied so you can watch *Sister Wives*.

Allowances

One last thing before we leave the sort-of crappy discussion of "money out" to focus on the happier topic of "money in": the allowance. Paying children money to do basic chores around the house – room cleaning, bed making, dinner clearing, garbage taking – is not a new thing. When I was young there was nothing better than jumping on my banana-seated bike, my un-helmeted hair flying free behind me, and racing to the corner store to spend my hard-earned cash on a chocolate bar, comic book, and maybe even Pixie Stix. It worked pretty well, from my perspective, and I think from my parents' as well.

I think kids today get a bum rap. While they are still expected to pitch in on family chores,[60] "experts" tell us not to pay them for "simply being a member of the family."

....

[60] Although some kids are not expected to do anything around the house, paid or otherwise . . . an entirely different problem.

In my humble opinion, these "experts" are slightly demented. This is not the way the real world works. Employees don't work for free, do they? Ah, but you might suggest that employees have *chosen* to be at work. Is it better to have the choice? Those of you who don't have teenagers may not have had it recently pointed out that they "didn't ask to be born." And certainly not into your family.[61] Since we can't legally send our kids to work outside of the house (I checked; honestly, there are no loopholes in the child labor laws), we are their sole source of independent income until the age of about sixteen, aside from the dollar or two Granny might slip them every now and again. I once knew a guy who did give his young children an allowance – but then systematically deducted from their small payroll sums for housing, food, water, and taxes, so that they were left with almost nothing. He said it was to teach them a lesson. If the lesson was that Daddy is a nutjob, I think they got it.

What it comes down to is that the paying of an allowance is a personal choice. To help you figure out where you come down in the debate, here's a handy list of pros and cons.

Pros:

- Kids learn about the real-world concept of "work for money." The sooner they understand this dynamic, the better.

....

[61] Versus the Kardashian one.

- Kids have the opportunity to save their own money toward the purchase of things they want but you don't want to buy.
- You can easily bribe them to clean up their rooms, clear the table, do some vacuuming, and maybe even fetch a glass of wine every now and again.

Cons:
- The concept of contributing labor simply because they are a member of a functioning family is lost.
- Every chore in the house soon has a dollar amount attached to it.
- They might save their money and spend it on items you think are frivolous (at best) or dangerous (at worst).

Where do I land on this? Well, as the boss of my family, I believe in paying allowance. I know this is how the real world works, and I know that kids under the age of fourteen can't earn good money working outside the home.[62] Establishing an allowance based on a minimum number of chores, with additional chores for extra pay, is a good way to encourage kids to work hard to get more. Sure, I know no one "pays" you to do the laundry or make their dinner, but you knew that when you decided to get in the family way. I think the benefits of teaching your kids that a video game

....

[62] Legally. But check around. You never know.

equal six hours of doing chores around the house far out-weighs any hard feelings you might have on the subject.

If the idea of paying your kids to *do something* is still not sitting right, here's another way to think about it. Just like I think you should lose weight for *not* eating the foods you could be eating, I think kids should earn allowance for *not doing* certain things. I've given some serious thought to this idea and have come up with the following compensation guide. It might work in your home as well.

NON-TASK	COMPENSATION	JUSTIFICATION
For kids: not calling your sister a freak every time you pass her in the hallway, thereby avoiding the inevitable fight.	$0.10	Seems low, but there is volume to consider here.
For kids and/or Dad: not kicking over Mom's wineglass, which had to be placed on the floor because the coffee table is covered with a Lego kingdom that she dare not disturb for fear of a total mental breakdown (mostly by Dad, who mostly built the thing).	$100.00	The wine isn't that expensive, but knowing Mom's luck, this was the last glass she could squeeze out of the box.
For Dad: not going to the Home Depot and instead taking the two hours to build the world-o-Lego with the kids so Mom could finish her article on "Effective Time Management for Working at Home."	$0.00	Lower than regular babysitting rate, granted, but *you don't babysit your own children.* I'm making a point here.
For teenage daughters: not saying, "But what's the point of dying your hair? You're old and no one looks at you anyway," or "Those jeans just don't work on you, Mom."	$140.00	The price of the cut and color and, apparently, our false pride and dignity.

NON-TASK	COMPENSATION	JUSTIFICATION
To Dad: not asking, "What do you need me to do today?" on a busy Saturday when the house is a mess, the children are the very definition of the "great unwashed," and he's holding a Home Depot flyer in his hand.	$135.00	Cost of the waterproof cast he might need when he dodges the mop Mom throws at his head while he's distracted by the special on power washers and reversible hinges or some stupid thing he doesn't need and has no idea how to install.

Bonus Payments

So you now know my stance on allowances, but what if someone goes over and above and exceeds expectations? In the work world, these employees give 110 percent day in and day out, just hoping for that elusive year-end bonus. This stick-and-carrot routine can play out nicely on the home front as well. Bonus-worthy acts might include:

- complimenting Mom's accomplishments to her husband, her friends (particularly the ones she doesn't like very much), her in-laws, or the teacher who can't believe you haven't managed to get a single signed note in on time;
- complimenting Mom on how her jeans look a little loose on her this week;
- complimenting Mom (you're sensing a theme, aren't you?) on the dinner she just made and the nutritional choices she makes for the whole family. (Too much? Okay, just that one dinner comment is worth something – or just don't complain about it. That counts as a compliment around here.); or

- being the one to tell Dad he can't wear those jeans and that fleece jacket in public. You're cuter. He might listen to you;[63] or
- Being the one to tell Dad about the red-wine stain on the new white carpet. While Mom is out. Picking up carpet cleaner.

Basically, kids are very amenable to this type of ~~bribe~~ bonus. We pay them to help us physically (if you believe in giving allowance), so why not pay them to help us mentally? It's another one of those win–win situations.

Money In: Creative Accounting for the Home

How's this budget thing working for you? Are you all balanced? In the black or, heaven help you, in the red? If your expenses are outweighing your income, you may need to take some cues from the corporate world to generate more cash. Here are some tried-and-true "business-world" strategies for improving the bottom line.

Service Fees

These hated, oft-maligned, and misunderstood charges originated with the banks. Mostly, we have a hard time understanding why we should pay the bank to manage our money. I mean, really, aren't we doing them a favor by

....

[63] Pay you a different type of bonus to actually burn them, if he doesn't listen to you.

giving them money to lend out to people like . . . us? The same is true when you think about service fees we *don't* get for managing our own families. There should at least be a nominal fee for:

- pouring drinks that the kids never finish (and the glass they don't put away afterwards);
- suppressing the urge to say, "Well, your sister has a point. That was pretty idiotic"; and
- listening to the same Justin Bieber song twenty-seven times and not singing along even though you're dying to. What, you don't find that catchy? (You have "Baby Baby" in your head right now, don't you? You're welcome.)

Taxes

Oh, the taxes we have to pay: income, property, sales . . . I'd like to start some services-based taxes for my kids. A percentage basis is probably good. I'm thinking of things such as:

- **Silence Tax**: Every time I don't open my mouth and embarrass you in front of your friends, you pay me. Per minute.
- **Clothing Tax**: Not in the traditional sense, but in the sense that I won't wear that "*Je Suis Cool*" T-shirt in front of your friends, or out of the house at all. Each day I could have worn it but didn't . . . you owe me.
- **Food Tax**: Again, not what you're thinking. Each time I pick a meal I know you like, but the other kids don't, the food tax kicks in. I'll calculate the cost of the ingredients and throw in a little one-upmanship for you.

Credit Cards

I worked in the world of credit card marketing for about ten years. One of my positions was Senior Manager, Loyalty Programs, and later Director, Co-Branded Cards. A loyalty program on a credit card is a system whereby the cardholder earns points translatable to money back or redemption for valuable merchandise and/or services. The more "loyal" a cardholder is to the card (i.e., charges the crap out of it), the better the rewards get and the more your financial institution will love you. As the manager in charge of these programs, I was constantly being pitched by companies who were sure they had come up with the "killer" credit card loyalty app. They would range from the environmental to the purely phil-anthropic to the data-oriented to the ultimate in luxury card programs. The problem always came down to the fact that people wanted real, tangible, consumer-oriented rewards over everything else – over saving the planet, rescuing orphans, or even getting better health coverage. We like to think we'd _like_ to support these endeavors, but when it comes down to it, we don't really want to risk our elite status for an endangered monkey or the like. I wonder what my reaction would have been to pitches for a loyalty program where the tangible rewards are points that can be cashed in for things like babysit-ting hours, housecleaning, pre-cooked meals, chauffeuring kids, attending children's sports, or maybe even a personal shopper. We could call it the "Mom Card." It could also have features like grouping shoe store, spa, and hair salon charges under the "Necessities" column, a reduction in interest rate if you lose more than five pounds in a month,[64] and if it's a shared card with a husband, an alarm that goes off every time he uses it. I like this idea! You could set up your own credit and debit system based on scored bad and good behaviors. "Family Points" could be given and taken away, or cashed in. Throw some in for Dad too.[65]

Earning Interest

You want to earn my interest? One of the ways we can make more money from our own money is to put it into interest-bearing accounts or investments. Money makes more money, as the principle goes. I'd be willing to pay out "interest" money if my kids showed the least interest in making beds, clearing tables, using a tissue when a tissue and not a finger is required, putting the scissors back where they belong, shoveling snow, mowing the lawn, or bringing me a glass. When they come up with an accounting principle like that, I'm in. On principle.

Yes, yes, I know there are basic accounting principles. My father is a chartered accountant and my husband is a banker. Blah, blah, blah. What these fellows neglect to take into account (see what I did there?) is a cost formula that I have used quite successfully for years. This is your basic cost-use ratio, which makes all kinds of sense. Take, for example, a

....

[64] Seriously, think about that one! Two birds with one stone: incentive to lose weight and to not pay out more money in interest. Gotta make a call to some old colleagues.
[65] Particularly if you're into a sex bartering situation.

two-hundred-dollar pair of shoes. I wear them once and, yep, it's still two hundred dollars. I wear them twice and I cut the cost *in half.* By the time I wear them out, you're basically looking at a couple of dollars per wear. They may, in fact, owe *me* money at some point.

Children have a huge cost attached to them, but they do provide a certain payback (it's okay, you can admit it). Let's review them as they might appear on a typical balance sheet.

ASSETS	LIABILITIES
Post-baby-body explanation	Post-baby-body existence
Messy house explanation	Messy house existence
Excuse to get out of boring social events	Having to attend boring kid events (which are rarely licensed)
Always having someone around for company	Always having someone around for company
Excuse for eating Doritos	Excuse for eating Doritos

In the accounting world, we hear a lot of talk about "return on investment" (ROI), and debate over whether everything we do has to in fact have a healthy ROI. When it comes to children, we need to get pretty creative in terms of proving their ROI from a financial perspective. They are, after all, cost centers and not revenue generators.[66] Sure,

....

[66] Something I have pointed out to my own four little cost centers on occasion. When they figure out I'm insulting them, they're going to get mad.

we can all talk about how to put a value on a hug, a smile, a tiny voice saying, "I love you," a snuggle in the morning, or a grin from across the gym during a school concert, but the fact is none of these would be recognized in a financial sense. They are, however, (say it with me) priceless.

A final word before we move on: family finances are never easy to sort out, but ignoring them just causes stress and can be extremely detrimental in the long run. Meet with a bank's financial adviser if you have no idea where to start. Time well spent. And don't forget to work in that monthly shoe allowance.

PAPER, PAPER, EVERYWHERE

The details involved in running a business are stupefying; likewise the minutia involved in running a house full of children. In some offices, low-level clerks might complain about having to staple forms all day. I've done that. It's not fun. But at least you usually know where your standard-issue stapler is. And the papers you're stapling together are always filed and found in the same spot, totally uncovered by peanut butter or jam. In a home, if you can even locate your stapler, let alone find the right form for the right kid, for the right sport, on the right day, it would be a miracle.

There are lots of effective filing systems out there

– online or something physical that involves a complicated series of cabinets, file folders, and labels – but I've yet to find a system that can handle the challenges of not only having the correct paperwork submitted to you by the child on time ("Oh crap. It's at the bottom of my knapsack. It's due today."), but having it remain in a spot in your home office (i.e., kitchen counter) where it's easily accessible and hasn't been moved by your husband, who can't stop cleaning up things that shouldn't be thrown away but has no issue with leaving his dirty socks on the floor of your bedroom for two weeks. The creation of such a system is about as unlikely as those socks moving themselves.

In the face of these challenges, I have managed to come up with some personal guidelines for dealing with all the paperwork that flows into my house on a daily basis. It's my experience that most of this stuff can be sorted into three easy piles.

- **The Money Pile**: This pile consists of bills that arrive in the mail, forms for school sports, field trips, yearbooks, classroom equipment, college tuition, orthodontic needs, etc.
- **The Government Pile**: Licenses, taxes, and other riveting information that you must have organized at all times. These people keep track of us.
- **The Miscellaneous Pile**: Birthday-party invites (note that these never arrive alone; there are always three parties scheduled to take place within a five-hour window – a sort of weird polarization of torture time), report cards,

parent-teacher interview sheets. These are all delivered via the most unreliable courier system ever: your child's knapsack. Don't go in there yourself to pull these papers out. You never know what your hand will touch. Send in the probe/child instead.

It's a good idea to put some inboxes or file folders near the front door (or as close as you can get without wrenching your back on an errant shoe) where the kids can drop their forms to be signed. You can add the mail and other assorted sports-team signoffs to another "To Be Dealt With" file. Assign Friday as a day when kids need to clean out their backpacks – all paper as well as the contents of that suspicious, soggy ziplocked plastic bag that may have started the week as a banana.

Do what organized professionals would do and only look at a piece of paper once. Once it comes out of the "To Be Dealt With" file, it's a) dealt with,[67] b) destroyed, c) signed and sent back, or d) ignored via the recycling bin. Paperwork can get out of hand quickly, particularly the more children you have.

Permission Forms and Releases

Although often found in the Money Pile or Miscellaneous Pile, these forms deserve a special mention. You think the

....

[67] Try to keep up.

paperwork involved at the office in order to get a new pen is ridiculous? Just wait until you see the forms that come home from schools and day cares on a regular basis. For some reason, in most households, it's Mom who is the designated Form Filler Outer and Signer, so be prepared to take on this title, but make sure you're being fed the forms, and their insidious requests for $13.25 in exact change (no checks please!), on a regular basis to avoid the early morning search and scramble through Dad's blazer pockets for change. And a pen.

With everyone from school boards to boards of directors increasingly concerned about litigious parents and the situations their children might get into, waivers are coming in at a fast and furious rate. Permissions and releases need to be signed in order for photos of children to be taken on school grounds; the wearing of helmets on a school skating trip; a walk around the neighborhood to raise money for charity; a field trip; a bus ride . . . you name it. I'm waiting for the following releases to come out so we can make sure our little darlings are well and truly covered against any possible injury, mental or physical.

- **The sideways glance**. I give permission for my child to be the recipient or giver of the occasional sideways glance. A glance combined with any sort of facial expression does not in fact signify disdain, condescension, ridiculing, or bullying. It's a glance.
- **The F-bomb**. Teaching is a tough profession. As is being the janitor responsible for cleaning up vomit. If a teacher,

janitor, or any school employee inadvertently curses while in earshot of children, there shall be no repercussions. If the cuss is directed at a parent, there shall be a parent-teacher committee convened to ensure that it was in fact appropriate. Important note: Anyone on the parent-teacher council needs to be sworn at once in a while. They're on the council.

- **Clothing discrimination**. Upon occasion, should your child mistakenly wear an item of clothing that is deemed "uncool" by their classmates, they will not be subject to playground humiliation. Rather, they will be escorted to the Lost and Found to find an appropriate replacement. Failing this, duct-taping over babyish cartoon figures on a T-shirt is allowed.

- **Lunch sneering**. Whether the lunch is too healthy, too junky, too elaborate, too simple, too expensive, or too disgusting, children will be banned from making disparaging remarks about their classmates' lunches. It is a proven fact that this will cause either obesity or childhood eating disorders. I'm pretty sure.

But it's not just at school where a form could come in handy. Think about the benefits you could derive, as the boss, if you were to have your subordinates/children sign off on the following:

- **Non-disclosure**: Oh, these aren't just for ex-wives of Tom Cruise and former nannies to Brangelina – the non-disclosure can be an effective tool to stop your children from sharing family secrets with neighbors, teachers, and mothers-in-law. Nobody needs to know about the soda for breakfast, faked sick days to get out of family Thanksgiving, and that Sunday after Mom's high-school reunion when she didn't come out of her bedroom all day.

- **Non-compete/exclusivity**: A gentle reminder to your kids that they're on your side. If you catch them doing chores at someone else's house (even accidentally) while their own bedroom lies in ruins or your lawn remains uncut, invoke the clause that removes them from dessert rotation for the next month.

- **Morals clause**: Particularly important when one has daughters entering the tween/teen years. The clause needs to be printed and posted by the front door in anticipation of belly-baring shirts, pants with "Juicy" written across the butt, and the arrival of teen boys with "Ride Me" on their T-shirts.

- **Insurance:** Kids need to learn to take on responsibility for things – that broken lamp, those melted crayons on the suede couch, and that ding on the new car door. Annoyingly, children rarely have their own coverage or in fact any income at all, so payment should be made in the form of manual labor.

- **Misrepresentation:** "Your son is so polite! And good with babies!" Ever hear this and think, Are you sure that's *my* kid you're talking about? This release is not to disallow misrepresentation; it's actually the reverse. It's totally okay for kids to misrepresent their true selves when they're out in public. It reinforces the opinion that maybe you made some good parenting choices along the way.[68]

If trying to stay on top of this mountain of paper is getting you down, just remember this: should the right releases not be signed and duly filed, you might be the subject of a complaint to the human resources department. And that's something no one wants to go through.

SETTING GOALS

It may seem a bit odd to be talking about goals in a section on getting organized, but, really, it makes perfect sense. How do you know where you're going if you don't know where you want to go?

My twelve-year-old daughter has a white board in her bedroom on which she lists her goals. These have ranged from "save money for Xbox" to "Meet Dion Phaneuf." She's achieved one of these, and let's just say she didn't faint when it happened. I love her whiteboard approach. It keeps her goals front and center in her bedroom, where she has to look at them every day, but the whiteboard also allows her to change them easily. Flexibility is key; we certainly don't

....

[68] Good parenting always includes smoke and mirrors. Really.

want to find ourselves working toward a goal we no longer care about achieving.

While setting goals for your family might seem like a strange concept, there are benefits. As the boss of them, for instance, goal setting is a great parenting tool. You can point out to them that spraying one's sister with a water gun is not actually "on target" for the "Convince Mom and Dad to go to Great Wolf Lodge" goal.[69]

When I first decided that being the boss in my own house was going to be of huge benefit to me, I laid out a few goals for myself. These included what I would do with all the spare time I would have due to fewer meaningless arguments with children who were never going to win them; more alone time at night (since the kids would be going to bed on time, without argument, and staying there); and a faster dinner time (as a result of children using their employee filters when sitting down to food they neither like nor can identify).[70]

Here's how my goals look today:

1) Stick to the plan. You need to know what your priorities are so you know why you're doing what you're doing, when you're doing it.

2) Minimize wasted time. Schedule everything and keep everything on schedule. Embrace anti-procrastination.

....

[69] Never mind making a disparaging remark or barnyard animal noise behind Mom the last time she put on her swimsuit.

[70] Hello, did you read *Shut Up and Eat*? It's all explained there.

3) Have clarity. Make sure the kids (and your husband) know what the plan is and how they are expected to contribute. Make sure they know who's in charge, all the time.

4) Put *me* in the plan. Make sure there is always time to get to the gym and do other things to make myself look and feel good. Put it in the schedule.

5) Be accountable. For money and for time. Stay on top of the paperwork.

Now it's your turn. Grab a piece of paper, your tablet, or a cocktail napkin . . . whatever's handy . . . and think about what you'd like to achieve in a few key areas.

Identify what is important to you, and make sure to revisit your goals every six months or so. Think about:

- **Your house**: Do you require a certain level of clean? Take steps to get there, and make sure to involve the whole family. They need to know your expectations as well.

- **Your kids**: What type of behavior is expected – in the grocery store, at Grandma's, around the dinner table? They don't know if you don't tell them or know yourself. What are they expected to do around the house?

- **Your husband**: Formally identify who owns what chore. And then back off. If he does it a different (or less perfect) way than you would and it bothers you, take it back and find him something else to do. Do what you're brilliant at, and let him do the same.

- **Yourself**: Make time for friends, work out, have some down time. How much do you really want or need? I have a friend with six children. She openly admits she doesn't want any "me" time. She's focusing on other goals. Figure out what works for you.

- **Your money**: This has got to be the most popular category when it comes to goals, and it's an important one, for sure. Do you have something you'd like to save for? A vacation? A down payment on a house? Retirement? Awesome. What are you doing to make it happen? Have you set up a direct deposit into a savings account? Figured out how much you can reasonably set aside out of each paycheck? Met with a financial planner to see how much you'll need to live on, depending on when you retire? If not, you're not making any progress. Write down something specific (not "save money," but, rather, "put aside fifty dollars a month for trip to Hawaii") and then take steps to make it happen. Call the bank. Hell, you don't even have to call the bank. These days, you can do most of this stuff online. There really is no excuse for not getting it done.

  Once you've sorted out some of your own financial goals, get the kids in on the act too. Ask them to write down something they'd like to save for (a toy or an experience), open a bank account for them, and work toward having them do *many more* chores around the house (or, better yet, for neighbors, who kick in funds from outside of the family money pool) to get there. Start small so it seems achievable to them.

- **Your time**: Are you time-challenged? At what time of the day do you find you are most often late? For morning appointments? Mid-day? Evening? What is it that makes you late most often – you, the kids, "life"? Make a goal to be on time for everything. And by "on time" I mean at least a half an hour early.
- **Your health/exercise**: Write your food plans out, and get your exercise planning in your calendar. It really can be as simple as that. But know what you're aiming for (i.e., the GOAL) before you start.

The upshot is that goal setting is important for a feeling of achievement in accomplishment. Keep your goals reasonable and make sure to stay on target.

REAL-LIFE LESSON

I often hear of bloggers (particularly "mommy bloggers") complaining about not being paid for their writing or their services. This complaint usually reaches me via a circular blog about why they shouldn't work for free. I couldn't agree with them more. But if you work for free, you've just worked for free. If the writing is your number one goal, you've achieved it. If making money is, you haven't. Figure out what is most important to you, and if you can't find a way to make both goals happen simultaneously, you might need to focus on one at a time. No one is forcing you to write for free; you're setting yourself up to fail at a goal you've established for yourself.

MANAGE THE MESSAGE

Putting Yourself Out There, the Right Way

If you've made it this far, chances are good that things on the home front are feeling a bit different these days. Schedules may be running a little more smoothly. Chores may be getting done a bit more efficiently. This is terrific news: it means your Autocratic Parenting campaign is on the right track. Life within your own four walls is improving. Good start!

Oh . . . did you think you were done? I hate to break it to you, but your family doesn't exist in a vacuum. Every time one of you steps out the front door, picks up the phone, or tweets, you are interacting with the world at large. Just what kind of impression are you making out there?

In the corporate world, entire departments exist to make sure that any given product is making the right impression and engaging with the consumer in an appropriate way. It's a big job, but someone's got to do it: publicists, marketers, and advertising departments. At home, it's down to you, boss. And your "products" can be a bit harder to manage than a can of cola, a wrinkle-free shirt, or nuclear energy.

MARKETING YOUR FAMILY. SERIOUSLY.

We may not like to think that we actively market our own children. The idea somehow conjures up images of child labor, the *Toddlers & Tiaras* phenomenon, and child stars going off the rails (and to prison and stuff). But I'm not advocating the public marketing of your children for a money-making venture (although if you have a surefire way to do this, please send me an e-mail at kathy@kathybuckworth.com. For research purposes only, of course). I'm thinking more of the ways that parents try to pretend that their children are the best on the market. After all, anything in life is only fun if you're better at it than someone else, right? Before you dismiss this, consider the fact that one of the world's most successful brand marketers, Procter & Gamble, built their success on bettering others. Basically what they call their "formula for success" is making sure that their customers value P&G's products over all others, both in performance and brand association.

So let's consider the parent who, in his or her own way, follows this proven competitive-edge marketing strategy by saying things like:

- "My children are little lambs/angels/rays of sunshine/darlings/365-day-a-year-Valentines." In my experience, there's a reason Mom or Dad is spouting off like this. Their kids are just as rotten as everyone else's, but they think if they polish up the apple a bit, you might a) feel jealous or b) make the mistake of inviting their kids over to play so she can go out. Don't fall for it.

- "My kids never fight" or "They're each other's best friend." I'm only going to say this once: *all* siblings fight. It's normal, it's natural, and if they really are each other's best friends, you should stage an intervention for the sake of their future social lives – or they'll *both* be living in your basement fighting for equal shelf space for their action-figure collections. And who gets to sit next to Mom at dinner. Before they go to the prom. Together.

- "My kids love to help around the house, without an allowance bribe. They know how important it is to be real members of the family." Listen, unless your kid wants to clean my bathroom for free, I really couldn't care less. Also, we know you've chewed them out over this in the past, or discovered an amazing way to make them feel guilty about not pitching in, and you don't want to share that with us. Go ahead and admit you've subdued them into submission on the bed-making thing too. I respect that.

- "Well, I just won't let them be assholes when they're teen-agers." This statement can only be made by parents who have zero experience in raising teenagers, most likely when their child is still in utero or, at a minimum, not past the age of cuteness (about six months). This is known in the marketing business as "ignorant opti-mism." Okay. Maybe that's not a marketing term. But it should be. Think of the products that could fall under this category: push-up bras, age-reducing creams, weight-loss pills. They're all promoted based on unsubstantiated claims. No one actually believes these claims, but we all live in hope that one day it'll all work out. Much like the removal of "assholeness" from teens. Good luck with that.

- "She's so smart that she's bored in class. It's not her fault." Really. So, stapling something to the teacher's head or threatening to light another child's shoes on fire . . . these are the results of being too smart? And here I thought we were witnessing the early days of a budding psycho-path. Guess you must be smarter than I am too, to draw that conclusion.

- "We were offered the gifted program for our child, but we turned it down." Total and complete bullshit. I'm not saying that people don't turn this opportunity down for their children. I'm saying the ones who do never talk about it. They're smarter than that. That's part of the reason they turned down the opportunity to allow their child to have no social life whatsoever.

- "He needs to play hockey at his own level. It's not fair otherwise." Not fair to whom? To you, who won't enjoy the same bragging rights about the whole Select Team thing? I'll let you in on a secret: people with real lives don't care about the hockey levels. Only you do. Oh . . . wait . . . are you talking about the GHL?[71]

....

[71] Gifted Hockey League. Gotcha. No, there's no such thing. Calm down.

- "He never puts himself first. He's always thinking of his friends." *Hahahahahaha!* Sorry. *Hahahahaha!* Most of us never really act this way, let alone display this character trait as a child.

Now don't get me wrong. I love competitiveness, but it has to be honest. If you need to lie about your kids in order to make it appear as though they are "winning,"[72] you're making false product claims and ultimately damaging your brand.

I spent most of my career working in marketing, and if there is one thing I learned, it's that you need to protect the brand while respecting the customers. When dealing with a family situation, you need to think about your mission statement and your brand voice. (If you can't remember what that is, reread Step Two.)

Many large corporations use the brand voice when developing their product and brand positioning. If the brand could talk, what would it say? If the brand could wear clothes, what would it wear? If the brand could travel, where would it go? Brands have to remain "on message" at all times. You won't find a Tide advertisement in a bar, suggesting that their stain remover is the best for getting out sperm or cigarette-ash stains. You'll find Tide ads all over women's magazines or on TV during daytime talk shows, telling you how to remove those grass and dirt (and, surpris-

....

[72] And preferably not in a Charlie Sheen sort of way.

ingly, blood) stains that your amazing children have gathered as a result of simply having good, clean fun.

Having worked in a corporate marketing environment for many years, I'm well aware of the discipline and science that it involves. It is frustrating to hear social-media pundits imply that "marketing is everybody's job" and that it is not a department. It *is* a department and it *is* a specialty. Read on for an explanation of what it is, and what it isn't.

Marketing Explained

No matter what type of business you're in – selling donuts or construction equipment – the basic tenets of marketing are the same: product, place, price, and promotion. Even with the influx of social media and new, smarter, precision-targeted campaigns, this has not changed. So what if you can reach out and touch someone via Twitter? You still have to manufacture a product or service, and have it available, priced appropriately, and in the public eye in order to be successful. With something as basic as laundry soap this is easy to comprehend. But how do the basic marketing principles translate to the running of your family?

Product

What kind of child do you have? What kind of child do you want to have? In my experience, you want that awesome combination of cute, savvy, and smart . . . with a big healthy dose of nerdy thrown in, which will stand them in good stead in high school when it comes to deciding between smoking behind the bleachers or signing up for chess club. The sad thing is that, even as parents, you have very little say in or influence on how your child is going to turn out. Oh, you need to trust me on this one. Environment only goes so far. Doesn't every family have a "black sheep"? How does that happen? Sure, you can assist in the product development (otherwise known as "upbringing"), but ultimately nature will have a far stronger effect than nurture ever will.

Place

In traditional marketing, place refers to where a product is distributed, whether online, in store, in a certain department, down a particular aisle, or in a particular part of the country. Children, however, manage to distribute themselves everywhere. But this isn't necessarily a good thing. A toddler in your liquor cabinet is about as appropriate as a Christopher Hitchens's book in the Bible Belt. As the boss, you need to manage your distribution services. And bear in mind that the children will, in fact, want *you* to do the distributing – otherwise known as driving – for them every once in a while.

Before you devise a flow chart or something, it helps to know that a child's innate sense of distribution is actually quite warped. Think about the classic cartoon *Family Circle* (about the family . . . drawn in a circle cartoon . . . hello?), in which Jeffy would often take the most circuitous route (detailed by a dotted line) from his front door to the front gate, stopping to see every single piece of wildlife, nature, lawn furniture, neighbor, and dog along the way. That's how kids' brains work in real life. They suck at distribution, so you need to take charge. Find the places you want your children to be and take them there. On the flip side, avoid taking them to the places you don't want them to be. Plain and simple. Need some further guidance? Children should not be:

- at a restaurant that *doesn't* have shiny plastic menus, a talking mascot, or an Ebola pit to play in;
- at a cocktail party (unless they are in charge of coat distribution); or
- in the family room after prime-time broadcasting has finished.

Price

Kids are freaking expensive, and the return is totally in the toilet. There is no financial reason whatsoever to have children. None. Unless you have nineteen or twenty of them and whore them out on a reality television show or just outright sell them in volume.[73] I'm just presenting options. The average cost of raising a child in North America is estimated to be about $200,000. And that probably doesn't include those kids who play AAA hockey. As a good boss/parent, you will need to look beyond the traditional bottom line on this one. Think of this, perhaps, as a not-for-profit

....

[73] Like the Duggars.

business. Or learn to define profit in a different way. For example, compensation could include:

- hugs;[74]
- an excuse for why your stomach is no longer flat (please note, this is for women only); or
- someone to blame for your messy house (priceless).

Promotion

When it comes to kids, there's no promotion like self-promotion. "Mom, do you know what I'm the best at?" or "Hey, kid! You suck at everything! I'm way better than you!" Yet as parents we still find ourselves having to promote our kids whenever we get the chance: "I think he'll be a charming addition to your classroom," that sort of crap. I like to use a little negative reinforcement on the promotional side: "I totally expect that he might cause some trouble for you. Here's my cell number."

Turns out I'm not the only one who thinks this way. When my twelve-year-old daughter started at the senior public school her older brother and sister had also attended, she was asked if she was more like her sister (an obedient, enthusiastic student) or her brother (a joking, laid-back, casual student). She said, "I'm more like my brother." When I suggested that perhaps she should have gone the other way, she countered with "No, Mom. I'm setting the

....

[74] Okay, that was just funny.

expectations low. I know I'm more like Victoria, but I have some room now." Smart kid.[75]

Beware Bad Marketing

Did you ever watch _WKRP in Cincinnati_? I loved that show. And perhaps my favorite episode ever was the one about the Thanksgiving turkey giveaway. Les Nessman's reporting went something like this:

> "It's a helicopter, and it's coming this way. It's flying something behind it. I can't quite make it out. It's a large banner and it says, uh, 'Happy . . .Thanks . . . giving From . . . W . . . K . . . R . . . P!' No parachutes yet. Can't be skydivers. I can't tell just yet what they are, but – oh my God, Johnny, they're turkeys! Johnny, can you get this? Oh, they're plunging to the earth right in front of our eyes! One just went through the windshield of a parked car! Oh, the humanity! The turkeys are hitting the ground like sacks of wet cement! Not since the Hindenburg tragedy has there been anything like this!"

This is the best-ever example of bad marketing: innocent turkeys thrown to their deaths simply because the executors of the campaign failed to research whether turkeys can fly.

. . . .

[75] She worries me.

Clearly, this turkey didn't fly, but it is a great illustration (and fabulous business metaphor) of why it is so important to make sure that you know what you're doing before you do it.

How do we teach our children the difference between good and bad marketing? Especially when it comes to themselves? Here are few guidelines:

BAD MARKETING	GOOD MARKETING
Calling Mom by her first name, prefaced by yelling, "Yo!"	"Mother, may I interrupt? I promise not to take up too much of your time."
Wearing a T-shirt that is stained, ripped, or too small.	Not doing that.
Dropping the "F-bomb" in a casual way.	"Oh, my gosh" followed by "Oh, sorry for swearing."

Basically, adults will judge a book by its cover or, in this case, a child by its verbiage and clothing. They judge each other, and they judge kids. Try to come out on top.

Talk the Talk: Marketing Vocab 101

Before we leave the endlessly fascinating topic of marketing behind, allow me to say a word or two about . . . well . . . words. One of the greatest things that good marketers do is introduce ridiculous words and terms into the lexicon. These words don't technically exist (which is to say you won't find them in the latest edition of Merriam-Webster), but due to their cool, pseudo-technical quality, these words make us feel like we need whatever it is that they describe in our lives. Who can forget Halls with mentho-lyptus? Who the hell knew what that was? Yet, we had to have it. It worked. Glad Garbage Bags have Odor Guard. Well, that has to be good, right? I mean, we want to protect ourselves from the stench of garbage, and something called Odor Guard must certainly do that. What is it? I have no idea. But it must work. I've even heard marketers talk about "decisioning" things. WTF?

Clearly, we parents need some made-up words to help us feel better about our products too! How about:

- **verbalosity**: The ability to talk non-stop about nothing in particular. Who needs awkward silences? "She's got good verbalosity."
- **questionification**: Any situation can be questonified by uttering the word *why* every ten seconds. Answers are not required. Not correct ones, anyway. "Could you questionify that for me, son?"
- **insultomatic**: This feature is automatically turned on during the tween/teen years and is an instant reaction to anything parents say, do, or start to say or do. "Oh, her insultomatic switch must have been flipped."
- **dirtclinger**: Instantly attract soil, dust, mud, blood, and paint stains within a 150-yard radius. Operates on high volume when combined with newly pressed shirts and that one pair of good pants. "Sunday school! Dirtclinger alert on high!"
- **flushfail**: The inability to successfully flush a toilet and its associated contents due to excessive volume, sheer laziness, or lack of consequence thinking. "Come look at this – classic case of flushfail. Wear shoes."

- **pickfix**: Anything worth picking is picked. And . . . well. "He was on a pickfix rampage."
- **smellsivity**: A unique sense of smell that instigates a gag reflex when it comes to blue cheese, curry, and olives but doesn't kick in for feet, three-day-old underwear, or serious lack of teeth brushing. "Her smellsivity dial is way up today."

Of course, children have loads of awesome features too, and I could spew out words such as *hugability* and *cuteable* but that would just ruin my reputation. And risk having my kids develop "materreader" (the inspiration to actually read some of my books, which generally isn't encouraged around here).

ADVERTISING

In one of his comedy routines, Bill Cosby claims that the first law of advertising is to avoid concrete promises and cultivate the "delightfully" vague. That's funny, Bill, because the first law in parenting is also to avoid the concrete promise ("I swear I'll come and play that video game in five minutes") and cultivate the delightfully vague ("I'll be there as soon as I can"). Oh, I know. Advertising gets a bad rap. This has been true all the way from Darrin Stephens and his boss, Larry Tate, on the show *Bewitched*[76] – who, when they

....

[76] Awesome the information I have in my brain, isn't it?

weren't creating punny ads, were shooting golf balls into shot glasses, which were subsequently used for an afternoon drink – to the image we have today of advertisers as snake-oil salespeople. While I love *Mad Men*, I don't think it's done much for the discipline either. I watched an episode recently in which Don Draper came up with an ad campaign for London Fog, which he told his creative director about on a plane, and which they executed the next day. Now when I say campaign, I don't mean the brand strategy. I mean he planned an actual magazine ad. This would *never* happen. Not then, not now.

In the real world, the client (the company paying the ad agency's bill) would come up with the brand strategy, the product voice, the key messages, etc. Often, they would also indicate the type of media they wanted (print, broadcast, online, that sort of thing). That would be detailed in a briefing document, which would be distilled and interpreted by the suits (non-creative types) at the agency, who would then brief the creative types about the execution, the medium, and, most importantly, the budget. The creative types would come back with a half-dozen concepts, which would be filtered by the suits, honed down, and taken to the client. It's a painstakingly slow process, and I'm pretty sure none of these concepts are finalized on a plane ride, with casting starting within days of getting back to the office.

Do marketing and advertising have a place in our home lives? Perhaps more than we think. Bad advertising and inappropriate marketing strategies happen when we feel the message and the tone doesn't match the product and/or service being offered. Being authentic with our kids and with our communities is vital when it comes to feeling good about yourself, and it can help stop us from feeling that we're not doing our best for ourselves or our kids. I'm all about Confidence Parenting. It helps to maintain a boss strategy.

So, what does advertising mean at home? Does it make sense to even think about the two concepts in the same sentence? Why not? If advertising is all about getting people to buy what you are selling – your "product" – then the average family could use a good campaign or two! You already know your family brand, so making sure the advertising lines up can be extremely helpful and is a good place to start. Now, not many families would take out a network spot or a highway billboard asking "So what do you think of us so far?" and featuring their perfect, media-friendly families.[77] Instead, we rely on word-of-mouth advertising. What are the neighbors saying about you? Are you the socially responsible family who just got caught driving home a brand-new Hummer? The nutritionally sanctimonious group going through the KFC drive-thru? Or the parenting writer with the tantruming ten-year-old?[78]

Applying the right creative strategy to a family takes some careful planning. The more fully we understand our child's "brand," the better we can manage it. A personal brand can

---

[77] With the possible exception of the Kardashians.
[78] Any similarity to my actual family is purely coincidental.

usually be described in a word or two. What words would you use to describe your children?

I have a friend with three children, and it was sort of accepted within her family that the first was the "smart one"; the second, the "sensitive one"; and the third, her "own person." When the school suggested that number two be tested for the gifted program, my friend was thrown. "I had compartmentalized him somewhere else," she told me. I found that really interesting. I do the same thing with my kids, and it can be dangerous. Kids are not products; their brands can evolve. If we start pigeonholing our children because of their behavior, it can affect them and make them become "that kid who always gets sent for a time-out" or "never meets expectations." The sell-ahead advertising on a child is evident at the school too, where teachers compare notes prior to the school year starting (they all do it). If your child is labeled (or branded) in a derogatory way, they're starting at a disadvantage. Resist the urge to label your kids or say things like, "But you know Sarah," particularly when Sarah is standing right there.

Companies work very hard to establish the culture and the tone of their messaging. But you can't *tell* customers what you are. It's something they have to feel in every transaction they have with you – from an online experience to the customer service interaction they have in the physical world. The same is true of us in our own worlds.

A Bit About Your Own Advertising

When I first entered the world of the stay-at-home moms (SAHMs) some ten years ago, I found myself, like many other SAHMs, sitting in a Starbucks. A neighbor of mine came in. She was a tennis mom and had her young son in tow. She stood out like a ray of sunlight in a sea of gloom.[79] Why? She looked fabulous. And, no, she wasn't in tennis wear. She had on fashionable jeans, a beautiful leather blazer, fashion boots, and a crisp white blouse. She had a bit of makeup on and her hair pulled back in a simple but classic ponytail. And I thought, Wow, *that's* the type of stay-at-home look I want to cultivate too. She was advertising the fact that she:

a) had it all together and had put thought into what she looked like;

b) took the time to take care of herself; and

c) cared what other people thought about her look, even if she was just running around doing errands.

I know some moms who resent the pulled-together moms at the playground, in the school yard, and at children's sporting events. I don't understand this. Of course, we don't always have time to look our best, or even to want to bother with it, but can't we be happy for others when they can?

....

[79] Mom jeans and fleece.

If you resent these other moms, ask yourself why. Do you think she's neglecting her kids by taking an extra twenty minutes to look good? Is she showing off? Narcissistic? Trying to impress the teacher? Maybe she's just taking care of herself first sometimes. Isn't that something we should all try to do? Sometimes? What's the message she's sending? As moms, we need to make sure the message we send is comfortable and relates back to our own personal brand. When the disconnect happens, the discontent happens. Take the time to be who you want to be.

PUBLIC RELATIONS

Public relations in the business world is a highly specialized art and science in which professional "spin doctors" work tirelessly to manage crises, spread their message, and keep their clients out of jail and off the front page of the news- paper, unless they're getting married or accepting an award. Hmmm. Sounds like the description of motherhood, doesn't it? The person who said there is no such thing as bad PR clearly never spent a minute hanging out in the school yard, where the slightest whiff of your child having done something awful (like saying, "Shut up") will taint them for a good portion of their youth. You must manage the fallout and keep the message from spreading in the "Mummy Media." The Mummy Media has a long memory and a short fuse.

While a large part of running your own family requires keeping things straight internally, sooner or later something's going to go public. And then you and the little buggers are going to have to face the outside world and subject yourselves to the type of judgment that can only come from other parents, teachers, and so-called authority figures. It is at this point that you will realize how and where you have failed to meet the lowest standard of what is expected of your child. It is also at this point that you will learn the value of "spin."

Enter a public relations strategy for your family. Basically, "spin" is the ability to shift or maneuver the press (the Mummy Media) in such a way as to make a potentially bad and damaging situation look like something you not only planned for but prefer. Action X wasn't a mistake! Action X is the way we do things around here, and everyone should be hopping right on that bandwagon. Allow me to demonstrate:

- "Why, no, Jimmy isn't color-blind. He's simply experimenting with shades and tones in order to gauge the reflective response of his classmates. In fact, the way your son is cringing at the mix of neon orange and green suggests that his color-reflex orientation could use some fine-tuning. Perhaps I can suggest a few techniques."
- "I think it's just terrific that my son is taking time off school to put some good, solid thought into his next move. So many kids jump right into a university or college program that just doesn't suit them! Just look at

the time [theirs] and hard-earned money [yours] that's been wasted."

- "Sure, the school Michael is attending has a reputation for dealing with 'problem students' and drugs. I thought it would be good for them to have him as a strong moral compass. Poor lambs."
- "Of course we allow Sienna to eat with her hands. It's part of a new food movement designed to introduce children of all ages to the historic methods of food feeling and texture tasting. You haven't heard of those? Gee, I hope your daughter doesn't pierce her tongue with that environmentally unsound plastic fork she's using, or pierce her tongue in general. That could happen too, you know."

Are you getting the picture? Spin is what's at work when we use words such as *spirited* (translation: freakishly annoying and loud), *independent* (has no friends), and *unique* (not terribly attractive, or freakishly annoying, with no friends) to describe our children. One particularly overused technique is the constant repetition of the phrase "My kids are so awesome." Just because you keep saying it doesn't make us believe it. On the other hand, it doesn't really hurt, unless the kids believe it too.

In the interest of educating my dedicated readers regarding the world of family PR, I offer a public relations primer. Sort of a *See Dick Shine*, if you will.

The Press Release

A press release is a public memo commonly put out by a company, either directly or via their public relations agency, to announce some good and/or important news about the company and its products or services. Press releases can be defensive ("Our product is still good for some people who won't die from it") or offensive ("Their product kills more people than ours") and can be a major damage-control mechanism.

If you want to imagine what a family press release might look like, just go back and review any of the "holiday letters" you received from friends this past year. You know, about how little Jacob was "challenged" in school (i.e., flunked out), or how Janie is "finding her own way" (i.e., unemployed), or how Pedro remains "attached to his family" (i.e., still living in the basement at age thirty-five). A word to the wise: the family holiday letter/press release that talks only about recent home renovations (complaining about how strenuous it was to live through[80]) and "once-in-a-lifetime trips" that happen every year is a sign that you shouldn't be inviting these people to your home anytime soon.

The Press Event

A press event is a public way of presenting a press release to a (hopefully) interested and influential audience. It will

....

[80] It's hard to watch someone else work, apparently.

often include a celebrity spokesperson vaguely connected with the product or service, a "photo op" (see below), a podium, a microphone, and some muffins. Media are invited to a public and usually affiliated location and, in exchange for said muffins, expected to report or review the subject of the announcement. A corporate example might be the announcement of a new car innovation at one of GM's manufacturing plants. A family example might be announcing little Jimmy's triumphant toilet-training completion, in front of a landfill, and later documented, with photos, on a personal Facebook page.

The Photo Opportunity

When an announcement is being made, or a product introduced, the public relations firm will organize the "opportunity" to watch the two CEOs shake hands, the faded sports star use the new lotion, or the shovel hitting the dirt for a new building. These planned, posed photos will often accompany the press release.

Amateur sporting events for children are the very definition of photo ops, particularly when the children are younger and they really haven't achieved much of anything on the field or on the dance floor. They're basically there just so we can get pictures of them in their uniforms/outfits. This is especially true of dance, where you're expected to fork out hundreds of dollars for an outfit they'll wear on stage for five minutes, after being photographed in it. You'll also have the option to buy the

DVD of the whole thing later, if you'd like. The outfit is good for nothing except maybe a guest appearance on *Toddlers & Tiaras*.

Regular family life often features photo ops during holiday and birthday celebrations, where the kids are too hopped up on cake and ice cream to fight with each other. Someone's hair will always be sticking up, and it'll be the worst possible picture of Mom. Oh wait, Mom is never in the picture. Never mind. A photo opportunity is a great way to get a shot you can post on Facebook or Twitter, just to show other people that your life is significantly better and more photo-worthy than theirs.

The Media Opportunity

A media opportunity typically occurs during a television show or radio segment. For instance, if you turn on *The View* or any daytime show, and they're talking about their "top-ten Christmas gifts," you have to know that each and every product featured is there because the manufacturer has sent either a media kit (with a release and probably a photo) or their product itself, and they would be willing to pay to have their product mentioned, or have their spokesperson interviewed about a mildly related subject, with a product mention dropped in. Media opportunities are, of course, less frequent on the home front (trying to get into the newspaper, unless it's for good news, should be discouraged), but it is something to consider the next time you have a birthday party in an indoor playground. Talk to the owners about what it would be worth to them if you gave a good review of their place in social media. Don't think of it as corporate blackmail. At least not for long.

The Segment Interview

A segment interview is normally heard on a radio or television program. It lasts between three and seven minutes, and the spokesperson being interviewed will attempt to drop a product or service mention into the first thirty seconds (no matter what question is being asked), so they can collect their paycheck and then relax and chat more freely during the remaining two minutes. Watch any actor promoting a film; they're masters at this. Frankly, I think we should train our children in the art of a segment interview so that when we're grilling them about who broke the vase, and we know it's them, they'll cut right to the chase and admit it instead of making us work for the confession. State your case and move on. Of course the best "network" out there is the "coffee date" with other moms. Set something up with a trusted friend (or at least one you trust this week) and have her interview you in front of other moms: "Oh hey, Kathy, how's your son's grade-four year going?" "Oh, did you hear about the award?" That sort of thing.

The Influencer

The word *influencer* has gained popularity with the rise of social media. There are, in fact, people who put the title of

Social Media Influencer on their business cards.[81] These individuals are seen to have some power or sway on Twitter or Facebook, and by recommending a product or service (paid or not) they can help boost the profile or sales for this company. The social media influencer of today is really just a person who has the ability to tap into the always powerful and longstanding strategy of word of mouth. Instead of leaning over the fence while we hang out washing, we're spreading our thoughts and opinions to a wider audience instantly. The challenge is that an influencer can, on occasion, lapse into what I like to call "brand bullying" – telling their audience that a company, product, or service, is 100 percent evil simply because they had a bad experience. This is terrible. It's like one child telling the entire school that your child is a bad seed because of one interaction. Advice is one thing; slagging someone or something off for personal revenge is another.

The same holds true for you, boss. Children (employees) are always listening, and if you expect them to respect your opinion on what you're telling them about how to behave, they will also (inadvertently) be listening when you start gossiping about teachers, other moms and dads, and neighbors. Make sure you are prepared to stand behind what you say because odds are high that your kids will feel the need to share any negative comments you've made about these people with these people at some point. They will also

....

[81] Stay away from these people. They can't even influence their children to make their own lunch, from what I've seen.

share this information with their friends, who pass it along to their parents, the school, etc. At best you might be embarrassed by what you've said; at worst you could affect someone's career or reputation. You know how much you hate those ads where they trash one product to make another look better? It's similar to that. Don't do it.

The Brand Mention

The brand mention happens within a media opportunity – whether that opportunity is on television or radio, in a blog, in print – and is of course worth something to the public relations firm representing that brand. For instance, instead of hearing that you should "wash your clothes in cold water" as an energy-saving tip, you might hear a spokesperson say, "I wash my clothes in Tide ColdWater." The mentions can be brief and pseudo-related to the topic being discussed, or they can be broader and more in-your-face, with an actual product in the segment. In the parenting world, brand mentions are often done by children whose parents believe that "who" they are wearing is just as important as "what" they are wearing, or what car they're driving. There's nothing more pretentious than a child speaking about the many features of Mom or Dad's new sports car. Try to keep brand names out of conversations with your children for as long as you can. With your friends too. Unless you're getting paid.

A positive "brand mention" for your family can happen anywhere – in the school yard when your child is pointed out for positive behavior for doing well in the classroom or even while playing at a friend's house. We know how it feels to hear that someone else thinks your child is doing something right. It's like a brand recommendation. Feels good.

SOCIAL MEDIA

Social media is an interesting combination of the modern parenting and corporate mosaics. When it's at its best, social media can provide us with insight, conversation, and engagement – whether we're talking to clients, consumers, or children via Facebook status updates, a quick Twitter observation, or a blog-comment exchange. Ramon DeLeon, who is a managing partner of six Domino's Pizza stores in Chicago, says, "The only way to put out a social-media fire is with social-media water." What does this mean? It means that in order for social media to work, you have to engage. I know, I know. That's a horribly overused term, but it's true. You have to engage in conversation, and engage with your customers/friends/family, in order to reap the benefits of social media and, just as importantly, in order for it to be contained.

Want to know if your college-age son is drinking? Check his Facebook page. Want to know if that person you saw speak at last month's conference is still getting paid to do that? Check her Twitter stream. Want to know if that Mom Blogger Vigilante still gets upset about formula, fast food, and Facebook privacy laws? Look at the comments she's making on corporate blogs, across the Internet universe.

Using social media tools across properties can give us a fuller picture of a situation; but remember that others can also use it to see what you're doing with your day, every day.

Making Social Media Work for You

Just in case you've been living under a rock and somehow missed this whole phenomenon, let's backtrack and clarify what we're talking about here. *Social media* is a term generally used to describe information and conversations that happen in the digital space, through recognized "socially" enabled services/tools such as Facebook, Twitter, Google Plus, foursquare, LinkedIn, and, once upon a time, the much-maligned MySpace.[82]

Here's a quick rundown of what you need to know about each of these social media sites and experiences and some tips on how you can use them to help manage your family in much the same way that corporations are using them to manage their message. Basically, there is no better place to be the boss of your kids than in the world of social media. It's a privilege, not a right, for them to be there. Use your common sense and monitor them.

Facebook

Facebook is more than just a site or a service, it's now a verb: "Hey, I Facebooked ya last night – why didn't you get back to

....

[82] Also I need to mention Pinterest. There. I mentioned it.

me?" Its traditional uses include allowing teenagers to show off their coordination, questionable drinking skills, and ability to dress themselves without exposing something, but it has grown to be much, much more. Take, for instance, the concept of Facebook Creeping. As a parent, this is a valuable management tool when it comes to finding out what your children are doing that they consider being brag-worthy. In other words, things they shouldn't be doing and don't want you to know about. There are several ways to gain access to your children's Facebook status pages without them knowing.

- Create their accounts when they are very young (i.e., under the "recommended" and legal age of thirteen) and set the password yourself. They might not realize they need a password to get in, and that you're always in there looking.
- Gain access to a friend or younger sibling's Facebook page/password and then look at your other child's wall to see what he or she is up to.
- Make them give you their password or friend you, or take away their smartphone. You're the boss of them, remember? (Go check the book title again if this is confusing you.)

Should you discover any unsavoury material on their page – which could include drinking, damaging public property, tattooing, or, worst of all, dissing their mother – punish them without explaining why. This is a perfect opportunity to pull out the "If you have to ask why, then you truly must think I am stupider than I am." (You may not want to use *stupider* in this particular context.) Creep their friends too, and tell on them to their parents. They're the boss of their kids too, remember? Honestly. Keep up.

Twitter

No, it's not (always) about what people are having for lunch. But it could be, and some people would still read it. How to use Twitter in the world of parenting? Well, Twitter can provide loads of valuable advice from others who have either been there or who are literally there right now. You know the old saying about only asking for advice when you want confirmation of what you already know you're going to do? Twitter is like that. Only on speed. "Should I clean my house or pour myself a glass?" Your tweeps won't let you down.

The biggest mistake I see parents making on Twitter is tweeting too much about their kids. It can be a) a violation of their child's privacy, b) too whiney/complaining about how hard it is to be a parent (wah, wah, wah, like, who knew?), or c) *boring*. Not every thought has to be shared on Twitter. Really.

Google Plus

Basically a more censored version of Facebook that allows you to share updates only with certain circles of friends, acquaintances, or people who want to be connected with you. You name a circle and put people in it. You can name the circle "Freaks I don't know" if you want to; they'll never know. At least that's what I was told and, boy, am I in trouble if this isn't true. Anyway, you send updates only to the circles you want to, thus avoiding boring your family and friends with your latest article (just me?) or sending those revealing holiday snaps to the accounting department. Oops. For instance, if you have a friend who is continually posting the latest hockey tournament results for her twelve-year-old, AAA-hockey-playing son, you might want to name that circle "Don't Care and Shut Up," or something like that.

foursquare

This one I don't get. You can check in at different locations, no matter where you are, if those locations are on foursquare. I get why this is attractive to restaurants, retail shops, etc. Visit a location often enough, becoming the most frequent visitor, and you earn what's called "Mayor" status. I don't get why you want to be the mayor of a gas station or a church. Oh, but wait. Apparently you get points for each check-in. Which are worthless and wiped out at the end of each day. Nope, still not with you. What, are you my mother? You always need to know where I am? Give me a foursquare app that automatically checks my teens into places they shouldn't be, and reports back to me, and I'm in. Otherwise, I'll pass.

LinkedIn

LinkedIn is a bit of old-school media designed to link people through companies where they've worked and colleagues and clientele with whom they've had dealings.

Mostly it's used when people are job searching or looking for references. You send or accept an invite to be connected to someone on LinkedIn. Personally, I protect my contacts here and only accept invitations from people I truly know (i.e., have actually met and worked with in person). I'm always surprised to receive an invite to connect on LinkedIn. Here's why: either I know the person and I automatically think, Hey, I didn't know Jim was looking for work, or I don't know them and I think, Hey, I don't know you, so, no, I'm not going to be your work reference. It is, however, interesting to note how many people check your profile, and why. I actually like LinkedIn, and I think part of that stems from that fact that it is essentially a *good* news sharing center that's kept at a professional level – something that cannot be said about Facebook and Twitter, which tend to easily devolve into the personal.

A Word or Two About Restraint

The important thing to remember when using social media is that, much like parenting, you don't have to say or send every little thought that comes into your head. Remember before we all had kids? Remember how *boring* it was to hear someone talk about their new baby and the sleep it got and the poops it pooped? Surprise, surprise – it's just as boring on Twitter. In fact, the only thing more boring is people who respond in sympathy to the "My baby won't sleep" or "Should his poo be green?" tweets. Please don't encourage them.

Sometimes it's better to just know that you're feeling great, or bad, and not share it with everyone. Imagine you're in front of the person you are engaging with and not in front of the computer screen. Would you write out a sign saying, "My left boob is killing me" and show it to them? No? But you just posted that on Twitter for a bunch of strangers to read, about five minutes ago.

So what to do? You could decide to post all positive stuff and suppress the negative. But do that and you're going to get nailed with comments like, "Oh, your life is perfect." While we find it tedious to hear about other people's problems, there's a part of us that really likes knowing that other people have them. Often.

We also need to think about what we're teaching our children about the appropriate use of social media. Like most parenting ideologies, this involves teaching them the benefit of restraint. When they post something that is less than flattering, or borders on the immoral or illegal, it's kind of like getting a tattoo. It won't go away on its own, and getting rid of it can be a long and painful process that leaves scars. For life. Skip the naked beer-drinking photos, for instance. [83]

Six Social Media Tips to Pass on to Your Kids
1) You never know who is reading you. Even the most

---

[83] Them, and you.

passive of passive-aggressive remarks will sting someone, somewhere, and often not the intended target.

2) Complaining about other people, products, services,
and situations reflects worse on you than it does on them.

3) Don't post about being sick. First, it's unprofessional
and off-putting. Second, are you so desperate for sympathy that you are literally looking to rely on the (fake)
kindness of strangers?[84]

4) Try to focus mostly on positive thoughts. In person, there's
nothing worse than dealing with someone who is a constant "Negative Nancy." It's not any different online.

5) Whatever you're dealing with, people have been
through different and/or worse. Don't imply that you
have a tougher life than anyone else.

6) Sharing is good; over-sharing is harmful. Don't share
any of your own personal information (phone number,
address, the fact that your mom and dad are away this
weekend), and don't share anyone else's either.

So, as we can see, managing the message is an important
part of running a family in the twenty-first century. What
you put "out there" *stays* "out there," and acknowledging
that our public actions can have an effect on how we are
treated, and how we in turn treat others, makes us all act
just a little better, don't you think?

....

[84] A virtual "hug" is totally meaningless. Sorry to break it to you.

Of course establishing all of these new rules can take some time. How can you possibly fit this in to your already packed day? Sometimes we have to call in extra help, but knowing who, when, and why to call is vital. Just like a manager at work wouldn't hire a consultant without knowing exactly what the deliverables will be, the boss at Home Inc. needs clear objectives when it comes to hiring outside help. So, who you gonna call? Let's find out!

REAL-LIFE LESSON

In my work with public relations companies, we develop campaigns that include the blogging and the social media communities. I am often asked to recommend individuals for outreach programs. Good work that pays well for the right individual. I will not recommend people who are constantly on social media complaining about how busy, bad, or illness-filled their lives are. You're going crazy watching a two-year-old at home? Not sure I need or want to add to your burden. You're soliciting for extra funds to get to a conference? Not sure that's the profile this company will want to endorse. Talking about religion, politics, and sex in an offensive or overly biased manner? Most companies won't touch you. Drunk when you're doing any of the above? Awesome. Not. Remember, if you're using social media to enhance your business, make sure everything you post is enhancing *you*.

KNOW WHEN YOU NEED HELP

Learning Not to Do It All

There comes a time in every boss's life when a universal truth must be faced. Some bosses – the good ones – learn and accept this truth early on, and their lives are better for it. For others, the realization is slow to come, and some pain and suffering may occur as a result. So what is this truth? What is the secret to sane and rational boss-hood? It's so simple it's almost obvious: you cannot do it all. You. Just. Can't.

Do you need to say it again? The sooner you realize the essential, rational, logical brilliance of this statement, the better off you'll be. Moms are the best at trying to do it all, and the worst at blaming themselves when it isn't all done, all the time. So listen up. Of course you'll still have a to-do list that's a mile long, but you've now given yourself permission to get some help with that list. Ironically, the first place you need to look when it comes to getting that help is in the mirror.

LOOK TO YOURSELF

Now, now. Settle down. I didn't just waste half a page telling you that you can't do it all only to tell you that you should. That would be crazy, and I'm not crazy. You need to look at yourself not so that you can lump more things onto your already overloaded plate. On the contrary, the idea here is to take a few things off. How? By asking yourself if that thing a) really needs to be done or b) really needs to be done 100 percent, exactly, perfectly. What I'm talking about here is a quick foray into the world of quality control, followed by a lesson or three on the art of lowering your expectations. Stay with me on this. You're going to love it.

Quality Control 101

In many large organizations, quality control is a major strategic initiative. The problem with parenting, and kids, is that strategies are easily thrown out the window once that annoying thing called "real life" kicks in. As the Earl of Rochester once famously said, "Before I got married I had six theories about bringing up children; now I have six children and no theories." Children have a lack of understanding when it comes to the notions of "quality" and "control," in their demeanor, personal hygiene, work habits, and output.

Let's start with quality, shall we? There is little quality to be had in the following:

- A five-year-old's depiction of his mother and/or father in a badly executed art piece. Don't encourage him – give him a rating and tell him to use some perspective. My butt is simply not that big, and as for how large you made Dad's nose . . . well, just erase a bit off my backside, okay?

- Ballet class for 99 percent of the child population. Look at your kid right now. No, really look. It may be cute, but it's not quality. And that's okay, isn't it?

- First-time goalie. The first time my son played goalie (at age five), a girl on his team skated by and yelled, "You suck." In a truly inspired piece of retaliation, he wet his pants and the goalie pads she would have to take a turn at the following week. He never played again. No quality there. Funny, but not quality.[85]

- The way they wipe their bums, brush their teeth, or blow their noses. I've seen kids attempt to do two or three of these in combination. There's no quality here, trust me.

- Bed making, room cleaning, table wiping, and general tidying. All of these would be written up in a Quality Control Manager's report.

Luckily, one of the ways we have leeway in quality control at home (as opposed to on a production line) is through the realization that the concept of quality is . . . well . . . flexible. A true sense of control may come from simply

....

[85] About five years later, my son came across this same girl at school. He ducked out of the way so she wouldn't recognize him. I suspected that given the time that had passed, and the fact that he a) wasn't crying and b) wasn't walking around in urine-soaked clothes, recognition during this brief encounter wasn't actually all that likely.

lowering your expectations. A three-year-old is simply not going to be able to Windex a glass coffee table the way you can. But that's okay. You live with a three-year-old. How long is it going to stay clean anyway?

Here's a good example. I have very low standards when it comes to keeping my house clean. While I don't (really) think I'm at risk of being profiled on *Hoarders*, I also don't have an issue with:

- Knapsacks piled in the front hall. That's where the kids dump them when they come in, and that's where they have to pick them up when they leave. Heaven forbid I should give them a reason to spend even an extra minute in the house each morning! Plus, our front hall is quite well ventilated, so the stench of the week-old lunch is somewhat dissipated here versus in a tidy, enclosed closet. See? Always thinking.

- Papers piled up on my desk in my home office. I know where everything is. I really do. I even know where the six-month-old vaccination form, tax receipts for the gift-wrap sale, and the "lice checklist" are located. They're mixed in with contracts, articles, calendars, and PR folders. It's all good. I'm a well-rounded person. Flexible too.

- Shoes in the front hall. Again with the front hall. It's a microcosm of the rest of my house. Shoes come off there, shoes go on there. I should reveal at this point my personal dislike of slippers. The only way I'd enforce a "no shoe pile-up" rule in my house is if everyone (okay, not everyone, just people over the age of twelve) agreed not to wear slippers in my presence. They make women look frumpy and men look wimpy. I need to post a rule about that in the company staffroom . . . I mean kitchen. Because if there's one place that kids will notice a sign, or at least stare vacantly at, it's on the refrigerator. Use this knowledge to your best advantage.

- The entire upstairs of my house. A close friend once said to me, "I've never seen the upstairs of your house." And I said, "Of course you haven't. Why would you need to?" Up there I'm hiding a bathroom from the 1970s, the fact that I don't force my kids to make their beds (I make my own and that's good enough for me, as on a certain level I agree with their argument that it will just need doing again the next day), the bag of clothes waiting to go to charity (which has been there for so long that I should probably dig through it to make sure certain things haven't come back into style), and the detritus that four children can leave in their wake as they walk from bedroom to bathroom and back again. And, no, we don't have a design on our carpet. That's blue toothpaste gel. It's vintage too.

Okay, so now you know my weakness (or one of them, at least). My house isn't ever going to be featured in a home-decor magazine. I've never even stepped into a home-design shop, to the best of my knowledge. But ask yourself this: is it really a weakness or is it a brilliant management tactic? I vote for the latter. One of the best ways to manage your time/workload is to take some of the pressure off yourself.

I cringe every time I see an article titled "The Ten Ways I'm Going to Be a Better Parent." The inherent suggestion is, of course, that we're not doing our best already. And we are. We really are. And that's the bottom line. You don't have to be perfect; you just have to do your best. Your best could be my worst, and my best could be your worst . . . it doesn't matter. Once you know that, things get easier. So why not consider implementing some new quality-control standards around a few other common household annoyances?

Meals

Yes, I wrote a whole book about this, but the basics bear repeating. The recent influx of food and cooking shows has made us feel that we need to produce three perfectly balanced and beautiful meals for our children every day. This is simply not possible and not (frankly) the best use of our time. I'm not saying we don't need to care about our kids' nutritional needs. We do. But if you want to take your kid in for a fast-food meal once in a while because it's the only chance they'll get to eat anything before you get them to that hockey game, well, that's just real life. And if getting them to the hockey game means they will be emotionally and physically excited and challenged, that's a pretty good trade-off.

I think the problem we face with the "big meal" (i.e., dinner) is that we try to prepare it when it's actually dinner time. If we turned our schedule on its side a bit and made dinner when it's convenient for us (during the day or on the weekend), we'd feel a little less stressed. Oh, the kids don't like that frozen chicken casserole you whip out on lesson night? Too bad. They'll like you even less if you have to cancel their extracurricular sports next year because you spent that budget on eating out every night, and now they're too fat to fit into last year's equipment anyway. I really don't care what my kids like and don't like for dinner; you can ask them, they'll totally back me up on this one. Of course if I know they have some favorites I'll try to make those once in a while, but sometimes meals are put together based on logistics (available ingredients, time, and Mom's mood) as much as on likeability.

If you really think your cooking skills are not where they need to be to pull off the family meal night after night, you could consider taking a cooking course to learn some of the basics. And by basics I mean hard-boiling an egg (or is that just my husband?). Which brings me to a major pet peeve (and I know I'm not alone on this one). When I travel, I often return to find out that the kids have survived on a diet of mac and cheese, pasta, and more mac and cheese. The easiest meals in the world to cook. Now, I'm not fussed that the kids eat this for dinner once in a while. What bothers me is that the meal is the result of sheer nutritional laziness on Dad's part. He feels justified in feeding the kids this dinner because he knows that when I come home, I'll make sure their nutritional needs are met and rebalanced with the meals I make during the week. It's selfish. And annoying. If you're one of the dads who does this, smarten up. Don't make me be the boss of you too. If I'm not already.

Personal Appearance

As you saw in my earlier comments on casual day, I do think it's important not to look really bad. Or at least to feel like you look pretty good, or like it's okay if people are looking at you. I watch *What Not to Wear* on a pretty regular basis, and the message I hear from the moms on the show, over and over again, is that they dress in drab clothing because they don't want to be noticed. I think that's sad. It reflects how these women feel like they don't have anything at all to show off. We all have something to show off. If you're feeling like you want to lose some weight, make it a formal goal and get the exercise and meal plans in your calendar now. Haven't had a haircut in a year because you "just haven't had time"? Put it in your calendar *right now*. You don't have to be fully made up every time you leave the house. You don't have to wear makeup at all. But at a minimum – be it through your clothes, your hair, or your face – present to the world something that you don't immediately apologize for. "My hair is a mess," "Oh, look at you with lipstick on – who has the time?" or "I know I look like crap, but what's the point of dressing up? I'm all about comfort." If you enter a room leading with an apology for how you look, people are going to know that you feel as though you're failing yourself. And that's not quality. Control what you can (i.e., yourself). Some basic rules in this department:

- Look in the mirror. Not the small one in the bathroom, but the full-length one that shows the entire outfit. People will see your entire self when you go outside. Here's a hint: if you cringe, go change. Something. Anything.

- Ask your teenage daughter what works. Teenagers of the female persuasion are nothing if not honest.
- Don't wear something that you have borrowed from another family member. Full stop. It's either too baggy or too young for you.

Homework

Let's break this down a bit, shall we? Homework is work to be done at home. Whether it's work that should have been done in the classroom or work specifically designed to be done at home, there's one commonality that all children's homework shares: *it's their homework.* They need to do it. You doing it for them is like having the supervisor come over to your production station and doing your job while you watch. Resist the urge to have your child turn in perfect homework that's only perfect because you did most of it. If the teacher doesn't know where/how they are struggling, they can't help them in the classroom. Also, don't be a homework nag. You're not the one who has to explain to the teacher why it's not done, and you're not the one who misses recess because of it. Let this happen once and see how quickly they get the message.

Home Decor[86]

I had lunch one day with a senior vice president at the bank I was working for. Over our two-hour meal (as some bankers are known to enjoy), she lamented that she felt guilty that her daughter's bedroom wasn't the least bit decorated. I admit to feeling no such guilt. (The fact that she could have spent those two hours meeting with a decorator or picking out paint herself was not lost on me, or you, I suspect.) No guilt for me because the rooms are beautifully decorated? Hardly. Actually, the opposite. Sure, the rooms are painted and there's been a tiny effort with wallpaper borders and decals, but mostly the kids have filled their walls with posters and pictures of things that matter to them right now. Don't get me wrong – I love seeing other people's kids' perfect rooms (but is that what those moms do all day?), but the fact is, it's not important to me. It should be noted at this time that I suck at home design and decor – the only household item I've purchased in the past ten years is our theater-style pop-corn maker. Because it was important to me. My husband buys all the furniture, pictures, carpets, etc.. He likes it. I once picked a paint color *over the phone*.

Here's the thing: I feel no guilt at all over not doing things I'm not brilliant at. Did you catch that? Quality comes from doing the things you do brilliantly, in a brilliant way. The things that you suck at? Do them in a way

....

[86] Full disclosure: quality + home decor do not go hand in paint-covered glove with me.

that is good enough. Do what you're brilliant at and don't feel guilty about the things that you're not brilliant at. If something you are not brilliant at absolutely needs doing, ask yourself the following question: can I do it at a level that won't make me crazy but will be good enough? If so, have at it. If not, get some help. More on that . . . now.

LOOK AT THE HELP YOU ALREADY HAVE

You're the boss, right? And that means you have employees, right? Okay. Then ask yourself this: Are your employees working as hard or as efficiently as they could be? Are they helping you out, or is the scale tipped in the other direction (reread the section on homework quality control if you are not sure)? You know you've got a problem on your hands if you're running around like an insane woman while everyone else in the house is parked on the sofa, eating pizza and watching a *Here Comes Honey Boo Boo* marathon.

Stop running and start thinking. There are ways to make the division of labor a little more equitable, and a little saner. How?

Revisit the Job Descriptions

Are you utilizing your resources (okay, your kids and husband) to the best of your and their ability? Instead of making your kids do the same chores forever and ever, amen, find out what they like doing and what they are good at and let them pick and exchange those tasks.[87] Brianna is good at making beds? Let her own that chore while her brother Matthew takes on dishwasher duties. Not all employees do the same work; they have specialities. Embrace this approach at home as well – just make sure you get to pick what you want to do first.[88]

Quality control works best in a work environment when each employee and each piece of equipment is working at its maximum efficiency. Small children are very efficient at . . . um . . . wait a minute. Okay, children under the age of five are not very efficient at anything, but you can train them to _not_ do things as often as they might; for example, eating with their hands, changing clothes every five minutes and dumping their still-clean ones all over the house, running out of the house naked, and dropping the F-bomb when Grandma comes to visit. Quality stuff. Older children can actually be proficient at many household tasks, and should be deployed accordingly. Bribing them with money is fine, but more important is making sure they know which chores they own. A boss who has to nag his or her employees into doing their work would soon fire those employees. We can't do that at home, but other punitive measures can and should come into play – you can always find them a worse chore, can't you?

....

[87] Things they like that actually better themselves, your house, or the world. Not playing Minecraft.

[88] Drinking wine and eating bonbons might qualify. You make up the rules as you go, okay?

Training

"Oh, just give me that. It's easier if I do it myself." Ack. Don't ever say these words to a child (or a trainable husband) when they are mid-task.

One of the worst things we can do as managers in our own family is to do the job ourselves instead of training the employee/child to do the job correctly. In corporate speak, this is called "dipping down" or "micromanaging." If we micromanage our kids, the end result is that a) we end up doing everything ourselves while they play video games and eat pizza and b) they don't know how to complete basic household tasks and are ultimately destined to live out their adult lives in our basement, since they'll be too incompetent to hold down a job.

Corporate managers are expected to mentor and encourage growth. Micromanaging is the exact opposite of mentoring, and eventually even the lamest employee will start to resent her manager dipping down and doing the work she is supposed to be doing. While a child might not actively complain about Mom making his lunch when he's fifteen, he should. The lack of training by Helicopter Parents today is ridiculous. Not only does it cause undue work for the parents, it prevents the child from learning to do the tasks themselves. If you are reading this section while cutting up your six-year-old's chicken, please stop. Do both of you a favor.

Is It Working?

So how do we measure whether our children are learning to do things themselves without driving ourselves nuts by constantly checking on them? One of the methods quality inspectors use to ensure that products are coming off the line in perfect working order is "random sampling." I love random sampling. You don't have to check everything they do all the time; you just have to let them know that the possibility exists. Why do I love it?

First, because the expression actually uses the word *random* appropriately (unlike most kids, who don't know how or when to use it); and second, because it's a useful parenting technique. It is a) less work for us than continuous monitoring and b) strikes fear into the hearts of kids in a regulated way.

Allow me to illustrate: We use random sampling when it comes to monitoring our kids' online activity. I honestly don't want to read all of their Facebook posts, text messages, or e-mails. But I do know that we need to make sure they're safe online and not sending out our credit card numbers. So, I use a random sampling method of checking what they're doing. At any time, I can ask them to take their fingers off the keyboard and not change the screen so I can see exactly what they are looking at. It works. So far.

Random sampling is good for things such as making sure they're eating their school lunches (tell them the teacher says they can't throw anything in the garbage that day and see what comes home), what their friends are really like, and what they keep under their bed.

LOOK AROUND

Sometimes even the most productive and efficient companies need to look for help from beyond. That's why contract workers and consultants exist (well . . . at least contract workers). Families are no exception to this rule, and, luckily, plenty of help exists for those willing to explore the options – some obvious, some not so much.

Small-Time Management Aids

Before we call in the big guns, consider this. On occasion, a stressed-out mom might find herself needing just a little help. The situation isn't all that dire. You don't need re-enforcements – not yet, anyway. Just look for the management aids – some quite cleverly hidden – already at your fingertips.

Electronics

Yes, I'm talking about the much-maligned "screen time." In days gone past, we watched TV pretty much every day after school, and we had to watch what the broadcasters put on at that particular time, on that particular channel. Imagine! Today kids can choose to watch what they want, when they want. This is awesome. If you need to structure their screen time so it's not excessive, do it during the times that work best *for you*. This includes long car rides, when you're trying to get some work done at home, long waits in doctor's offices, and, let's be honest, the occasional church service. Embrace what technology has brought to us for our children; you still get to manage how they use it. This is a good thing.

Adjustable Pants

I know, right? From the latest in technology to pants. Little boys in particular are known for having no hips and teeny little butts. For generations now pants have been sliding down backsides to the point where teenage boys today are completely comfortable with the waistband down around their knees. But I have high (-waisted) hopes for the next generation. Adjustable elastic bands now allow pants to fit even the smallest of frames. Our new little guys will soon be comfortable with the feeling of material around their midsections, and mothers everywhere can stop taking in waistbands. Phew!

Suitcases with Wheels

Why did it take humankind hundreds of years to finally put wheels on suitcases? Just thinking about how we used to lug our over-stuffed luggage through airports makes me tired. This clearly works for adults, but the really brilliant thing is it works for kids too. Now kids can have their own little suitcases to roll along behind them (less work for you!), and, somehow, knowing that the suitcase is *theirs* has made kids everywhere embrace the whole packing process! Of course we need to make sure that essential medicines are on board, but we can pretty much bow out of the scene at this point. Make them a list, and have them follow it. They like doing it. If they can't read, draw three shirts – you can even draw the ones you want them to pack. It's this crazy thing called "delegation," married with responsibility, and it just might work. If they forget underwear on this trip, they won't forget it on the next one.

Smartphones

I go back and forth on this one. While it's great that we can use our smartphones to stay in touch with our kids, it's not so great that they can use *their* smartphones to stay in touch with *us*. When I need to get a hold of them, it's important. When they need to get a hold of me, it's usually to ask me to do something. I don't need them to have immediate access in one of those scenarios. According to a recent survey,[89] 48 percent of children aged eleven and over have a cell phone. Take my advice and teach them how to use this cell phone in a safe and polite way. Just because we blazed the trail by using these marvels of technology in cars, while walking across busy streets, and in the middle of romantic dinners does not in any way mean we have to pass on these rude and dangerous methods to our children. Help put the "smart" back in smartphone.

Social Media

The ability to reach out via Twitter and Facebook, to crowd-source information and, let's face it, empathy, is an amazing

....

[89] Presidents Choice Services survey of Canadians, 2012.

tool for moms and dads, new and old, who are dealing with something in their child's life for the first time. And we all know that happens pretty much every day. I love crowd-sourcing – it gave me a few ideas for this book. I've also been able to find out just how many moms are still making their kids' school lunches, doing their laundry, and driving them everywhere. And some of the kids are twenty-five.

Contract Employees

As helpful as these little advancements and technologies may be, often – too often – we find ourselves with more work than there are hours in which to do it. If this happens at the office, outside help is often procured in the form of contract or occasional employees. At home we routinely employ con-tract workers to take care of chores that we do not have the time or, frankly, the inclination to do ourselves. If you're not used to thinking outside of the box in this way, you may need to kick-start your imagination. Here's a rundown of some popular contract-help options to get you started.

The Babysitter

Watching children under the age of twelve takes valuable time and energy. If you have some disposable income (or money earmarked for "help" in the budget), and the phone number of the one fourteen-year-old in the neighborhood who doesn't yet have a social life or a real part-time job, you've got what you need to get some help. One of the first "outside hiring" jobs we do as parents is finding a babysitter.

This is encouraged. You need to leave the house without your children once in a while, and untended toddlers are not known for their sensible survival skills.[90] Top things to look for in a babysitter are availability, good hygiene (hair crawling with lice and open sores can be a turn off), and the ability to look at a dirty diaper without going all "Ewwwww" on you. It's not all that important that your kids like them; it's important they're capable and can do the job.

The Tutor

Unlike the babysitter, who is basically hired to keep the children alive and Child Welfare Services from your door, the tutor is expected to actually improve your child in some way or another. Whether for math, English, or foreign language skills, the tutor is brought in when a) Mom and Dad simply don't have the time to assist with homework, b) Mom and Dad don't have the expertise to assist with homework (usually kicks in around grade-five math), and/or c) Mom and Dad have both the time and the expertise but zero patience with the child who keeps laying his head down on the table and saying, "It's not fair" over and over and over again. It's good to hire someone who is still enrolled in school, or at least an individual who didn't graduate before the introduction of computers into the classroom. The whole "new math" thing isn't going to make much sense to

....

[90] Also, against the law. I checked.

them. Above all, hire someone who is smarter than you . . .
otherwise, just do it yourself.[91]

Cleaning Staff

If you have children, your house is messy. If you live in your
house, your house is messy. How messy you decide to keep it
is entirely up to you. Freeing up a revenue bucket as a resource
to pay for an additional level of cleaning can be a very good
thing. I will just say this: if you have money for hockey equipment, dance shoes, and art supplies, but don't have money for
a cleaning service, you're doing something wrong. You have
these extra things in your house making extra mess, and you
have to clean it up. Cut out the lessons, you don't need the
equipment, and there's less to clean up. It's sort of a win–win–
win.[92] I have four kids. I do not "clean up" before the cleaning lady comes. If anything, when breaking in a new cleaning
person (which is, now that I think of it, quite often), I try to
have the house at its dirtiest best; in the future, it will seem
like I made an effort. Hire a trustworthy person whom you're
fairly certain won't one day write an exposé.

The Nanny

You trust these lovely ladies (and occaisonal "mannies") to
raise your kids with the same values you try to stick to.

....

[91] Actually, never mind. Tutoring your own child at anything is painful. How about "at least
as smart as you"? Perfect.
[92] Unless you're the child. But you're not, are you? You bought this book, they didn't.

Having a nanny raise your child is a pretty good gig, all things considered. If the kids turn out to be fine, upstanding citizens, everyone will praise you, the parents. If they end up searching "fail" videos on YouTube for sixteen hours a day (in which they are featured), you can blame it on the nanny. Parenting always involves a good exploration of "where did we go wrong," and having had a full-time nanny offers an easy answer.

The Gardener/Pool Guy

If your children and husband aren't capable of keeping a pool clean or a plant alive, you are fully justified in looking for outside help. If you live in a warm climate, you might want to make sure that if a shirt is coming off, there's something worth looking at underneath. What? You're the boss, aren't you?

The Coach

I know. We don't hire a coach for our kids' sports teams. He or she is usually a volunteer, and is always responsible for the team in its entirety, not just for your child. But the coach is an adult whose voice your child actually listens to. So it can be important to know what a good coach sounds and looks like, and what a bad one sounds and looks like.

- **Good?** Has a bunch of fun training drills ready for the kids, emphasis on the fun.
- **Bad?** Turns up late and tells the kids to "run around" and "shoot at something."

- **Good?** Wants to win the game but teaches them to be polite winners and not have a sour-grapes/sore-loser attitude.
- **Bad?** Calls the boys on a team "ladies," gets mad when they lose, and encourages them to punch or sneak in a few shots when they're losing.

Pretty straightforward, really. The coach explains to your child why sport is for fun and winning doesn't matter while simultaneously telling them to win the game. They also get to console them when they lose. It's complicated and probably should be a paid position. Add a line in the family budget for a good bottle of scotch at season's end. Poor sop deserves it.

Consultants

I've worked for and with many large corporations: Coca-Cola Foods, Telus, French's Mustard, CIBC, Royal Bank, Procter & Gamble, General Motors, Research In Motion, Air Canada, and more. Every single one, at any given time, has had at least one consultant on the payroll. Some contract, some "embedded" (for example, as in a public relations employee who works at the client's office full-time, providing advice), some as one-time project managers.

Many large corporations hire outside consultants based on the following assumptions:

- Only people not stupid enough to work in their organizations can figure out a new way of doing things. In fact, it's great if they don't have even a basic understanding of the business.

- Big, colorful diagrams full of overlapping circles, upside-down pyramids, and shifting paradigms are clearly the only way to get through to the morons who work here.
- Without a motto, acronym, or three-word cheer that ends in an explanation point (extra marks if it includes a pun), there can be no strategic shift. Or mugs, T-shirts, and pens that bear said motto.

Consultants do have a valuable use in the work environment. Mostly they are able to point out glaring dysfunctional areas that the entire organization is aware of, except for those in the executive suite. An objective view to changing things that have "always worked that way" can result in more efficiencies. Consultants are also awesome when it comes to having someone to blame after their suggestions don't work. They have moved on to another project by then and can't hear you implicate them in every other thing that has gone wrong in your area of responsibility as well.

At home, consultants are fairly rare, unless you're redesigning your kitchen or undergoing a personal makeover. This a shame, really. Off the top of my head, I can come up with several consultants who would be very useful. Pay attention, all you entrepreneurs.

Bedtime Consultant (i.e., Sleep Doula[93] or Night Nanny)

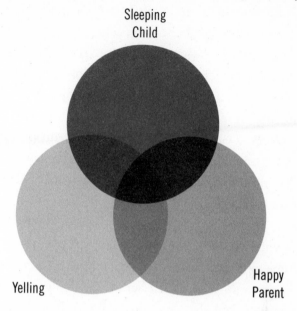

Sleeping
Child

Yelling

Happy
Parent

Problem: Your child will not go to bed. You have explained many times to your bored friends that he "just won't go to bed." This is false. He will. The sleep consultant can tell you how. Check the diagram: Put a child to bed, and he'll be back in five minutes. Teach a child to sleep, and you'll get used to sleeping with your legs curled up against the Thomas the Tank Engine frame. Talk to a child about sleeping alone, and you'll have the wrath of the Helicopter Parents on you. Delegating "putting child to bed/sleep" to

[93] Visit www.sleepdoula.com. She's a friend of mine.

the actual child allows the boss (Mom) to free up valuable evening time that can be used for reading, drinking wine, or actually sleeping herself.

Yes, that's basically about it. If you have a sleeping child, it means that there has been some yelling – either from the parent, or the child, and it has finally stopped, and in the end they can all meet up.

Lesson Learned: You are the boss of them. You can make them go to bed without having them feel like it's punishment; rather, it's a basic job requirement. There is no room for negotiation here.

Listening Skills Consultant

Problem: Your child never listens to you. You can look her straight in the eye and tell her to pick up her socks in the front hall, and she won't do it. You've had her hearing checked five times.[94] Why does the consultant's method work? Tell a child to listen to you and they'll say, "What?" A talent they continue to grow to its zenith at teenage-hood. Show a child good listening skills by not ignoring your husband's requests to hurry up and get ready. Show them the results of Daddy not listening to Mommy by booking a spa appointment during an NFL play-off game. See ya, sucker. Hear that? Bottom line? Everyone needs to listen to Mom. Check out this handy and easy-to-read chart.

....

[94] I'm using a female example here, but we all know it's the boys who are the worst.

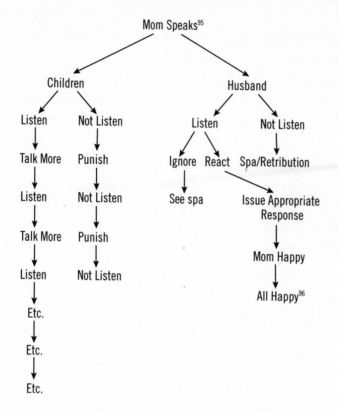

Lesson Learned: You just have to know the key motivators to listening for a child. These range from fear all the way through to deprival. I know it sounds harsh. There's no trophy either. But that's okay. You know why? Kids don't have to be happy all the time.

....

[95] We're moms. It's what we do.
[96] THIS IS WHERE YOU WANT TO BE.

Conflict Resolution Consultant (Boxing Coach)

Problem: "She hit me!" "He's spitting on me!" "She's an idiot!" "He's disgusting!" They. Fight. All. The. Time. Tell the kids to stop fighting, and they'll stop. For two seconds, until a remote control comes out of nowhere and hits someone in the head. Show a child how to fight fair and come to resolution, with your husband. Fake it if you have to. The resolution, that is. (Seriously, you know who's going to win.) Teach a child to trick the other person into agreeing with them, and no one need be the wiser. All kids fight. It's annoying to be the referee all the time. Let them fight and let them resolve. It'll save you all some time and frustration.

I'm telling Mom you ate the cookie without permission unless you agree with me. Welcome aboard.

I'm right and you're wrong. But if I give you a cookie, I could be right. Right?

You've eaten the cookie and reconsidered? Well if you disagree with me, you'll be agreeing with Mom. Thought so.

Lesson Learned: Manipulation and deceit are not just for the corporate boardroom. They work well at home as well. Use your skills, people.

Other consultants you might want to consider:

- Cleanliness Consultant:

  Problem: Kids are pigs. Put a teenager in his messy bedroom and he'll say, "What? It's fine." Teach a teen to clean up a room and you'll have just done it for them, while they smirk. Talk to a child about how the synergistic relationship between a clean bedroom and access to the car keys works, and you'll get results. Or your car to yourself. Win–win.

  Lesson Learned: Know the right motivators. "Because it's nicer to have a clean room" or, even worse, "While you live under my roof, you're going to respect my property," (yawn) these don't work. Take away a car. Or a girlfriend.

- Personal Hygiene Consultant:

  Problem: Kids are hygienic pigs as well. Tell a child they stink, and they say, "Thanks." Show a child how to brush their teeth, comb their hair, and put on deodorant, and they'll have just advanced a level on Call of Duty, which they were surreptitiously playing on their personal gaming device instead of listening to you. Teach a child about the relationship between good personal hygiene and the odds of them leaving the house to go out with friends, and they'll drive up Axe stock.

Lesson Learned: Find the motivator. Are you sensing a pattern here? No. Maybe you are the problem after all.

- Vehicular Space Containment Consultant:
Problem: They fight over where to sit in the car. Every. Single. Time. Tell a child to "Get in the car!" and watch the scrambling and punching and yelling "Shotty" begin. Show the children how you and your husband don't fight over who sits in the driver's seat versus who sits in the passenger seat (this is a bad example after a Christmas party). Teach the children to negotiate with their siblings and watch the little ones get tricked into the back row every time. Which is fine, because then the older ones have to help them with seatbelt issues, passing tissues back, and getting their seats kicked, instead of yours. Win–win.
Lesson Learned: Corporate manipulation wins again. This time you are mentoring it.

The long and the short of consultants is that they are there to provide you with advice. And, as Benjamin Franklin said, "Wise men don't need advice. Fools won't take it." Or as Bill Cosby said, "It's not the wise who need a word. It's the stupid."

Books, Games, and Television Shows

Every week there are hundreds of management books written and published, all of which contain perfectly sound advice that has likely worked at least for the person writing the book. Good for them. But do yourself a favor: instead of buying another guru's latest book, revisit your child's bookshelf or the children's section of your local library or bookstore. Many of the classic tales contain all of the management advice you'll ever need, both in the boardroom and in the family room. Here's a rundown of some of my favorites and how you can put their advice to work in your home.

Goodnight Moon

This perennial children's favorite contains one of the most-loved lines of all time: "Goodnight nobody." Because even nobodies deserve some sort of recognition. And I mean "nobody" in the nicest possible way. Be it the summer intern or the junior product manager, acknowledging an employee's existence is an effective tool for senior management. One day these "juniors" could easily be your boss. Also, they're smart and worth listening to. Some kids are as well. Some. Recognize *everyone*, and teach your kids that everyone deserves to be listened to.

Green Eggs and Ham

In this Dr. Seuss tale, Sam I Am tries to convince his hapless friend to try a new culinary dish, in a number of different settings: on a boat, in a car, on a train, heavens, even with a goat. I'm not a fan of this book from a personal perspective because it has the provider of food (in this case, Sam, but in most houses, Mom) running around begging for his pal to try a new type of food. Have you read my previous book, *Shut Up and Eat*? Don't run around after your kids. Just make them eat.

In business, however, we often find a solution by turning a problem on its head, by trying different things, or sometimes the same things in different ways. Make sure to take a run at a problem with the kids a few times before throwing in the proverbial towel. Parents who say, "He will only eat peanut-butter-and-jam sandwiches every day and there's nothing I can do about it" have given up. You can do something about it. You're the boss, remember? Pull out some green eggs if you have to.

Nursery Rhymes

So you think you don't know Jack about management principles? Well apparently Jack knew a ton of stuff, as evidenced by him turning up time and time again in nursery rhymes.

- "Jack Be Nimble." Jack wasn't only nimble, Jack was quick. He jumped over that candlestick and, one assumed, didn't get burned. He acted quickly and didn't ask his children how they felt about him doing it or for permission to land on the other side. Perhaps the earliest example of "Just Do It." (Pssst, Nike – seriously – put some runners on this guy and sign him up.) Follow Jack's lead.
- "Jack and Jill." So, they go up this hill, right? To fetch some water. Then he falls down and she goes tumbling after. The key here is delegation. Don't follow someone up a hill to get something when they can just bring it to you.

- *Jack and the Beanstalk.* While this is technically a book, and not a nursery rhyme, Jack is at it again. He trades a cow for beans, grows a stalk, gets rich, and kills a giant. You just never know what that first move is going to get you, but if you don't make the first trade, you'll never know. Go with your gut and parlay your experiences into a great big win(dfall).

- "Jack Sprat." He couldn't eat fat, so he married someone who would, a move that allowed him to have the lean. The takeaway? Partner up with people (and, yes, your kids count as people) who can do what you can't.

The Game of Life

Turns out it's not just children's books that we can learn from. I think some of the best management tools are board games. I often play board games with my children, and besides providing the opportunity to learn a bit of math, reading, and logic, the games examine that all-important role of luck. We can't always choose our own circumstances (or children, for that matter), but we can roll the dice and move forward. If you've participated in experiential training programs, you'll know that most are built around games. Why not take advantage of ones that we already know and love and save the consultants fee?

Monopoly

My childhood was filled with many rounds of Monopoly. Which always seemed to end with me, or one of my hapless siblings, sitting with one bad piece of property and about twenty-two dollars, while our dad, the real-estate king, gleefully waited for us to land on one of his monolithic hotels, only to tell us that he wouldn't charge us the full amount so he could keep the game going and prolong our agony. I'm not sure what lesson we were learning there, except that when you're winning, enjoy every minute of it. And winning is so much better if someone else is losing tremendously. The game itself teaches you to spend money to make money, and to do business with whomever you need to do business with. You might have been punching your brother during a snack break, but five minutes later you're doing a deal and combining forces to take down little sister. Monopoly is not for sissies.

Sorry
Totally a game of luck, with the only mitigating factor being that you can decide whom you will send back home, depending on your mood, and the best move. Sort of like when you have the kids out at a function and you have two cars. Pick a spouse, pick a kid, and send them home with a big "Sorry." Also, no one who ever played Sorry is ever sorry. They should really call the game "Booyah."

Clue
One day I'm going to invent a game called "Get a Clue" and market it to teenage boys, but that's another story. Possibly another book. The object of the game is to figure

out who killed Mr. Body, in what room, and with what instrument. It can be easy to get the right person, the wrong room, and the right instrument, but tricky to get all three. I think this game can teach kids about calculated risk (in guessing before you're 100 percent sure), waiting too long, and losing out because someone else guessed first on their turn. While it's important to have all of your ducks in a row, knowing when to make a calculated risk and move before all the evidence is in can make the difference between winning and losing.

Game playing requires a lot of luck. And dedication. Proving once again that Samuel Goldwyn knew what he was saying when he uttered, "The harder I work, the luckier I get." Pass the poker chips.

REAL-LIFE LESSON

One of my previous jobs was that of product manager, Classic Visa. About the only thing classic about this job was the many bureaucratic and outdated business practices to which I was subjected. It was a hotbed of micromanaging nightmares. I worked for a marketing director during a time when we were announcing the elimination of the card's annual fee. This was a bold move back in the early 1980s, and one that we wanted to announce quickly to catch the competition off-guard. She literally had the newspaper presses stopped and the ad pulled because she felt the card visual was not placed at a "jaunty" enough angle. We lost a day and another bank announced before us. Dipping down takes time away from your responsibilities and often messes up what's going on with theirs. Remember this the next time you're building a science fair project at two in the morning while the real student sleeps.

HAVE FUN WITH IT

Enjoying the Perks

Are you having one of those days when things are just get-ting you down? When your spreadsheets don't balance and your flowcharts won't flow? Could be you've been working too hard, and forgetting that one of the benefits of being the boss is that you can have a little fun now and again. Why not amuse yourself by going all corporate on their butts? What use is being the boss if you never take the time to enjoy the perks? Unleash a new policy or two! Start speak-ing in acronyms! Plan a family outing! Oh, wait. You may want to rethink that last one.

A CHANGE OF SCENE

The best remedy for a lack of energy and focus is often a change of scene. In the corporate world, this theory is behind the whole notion of off-sites, retreats, and other staff outings. Do these things work? Who knows, but bosses and executive boards everywhere keep trying, so something must be going right, right? But here's a better question (at least for you): Do these things work for Family Corp? Let's look at a few and see.

The Company Outing

Ah, the retreat. If you haven't experienced one of these beauties, you have no idea what you're missing. If, on the other hand, you have worked in a large corporation or two, you know the hell of "experiential learning" and "team-building exercises." That's right – you've probably built a skyscraper out of cardboard boxes and fallen backwards off a picnic table into the arms of the team you trust. As if that isn't painful enough, you're expected to find some meaning in all of this that you can take back to your everyday office life and job, which has just gotten even worse due to the fact that you're now eight hours behind in e-mails, meetings, and report writing as a result of this "off-site." The idea is that life informs work and work informs life and . . . yeah . . . well . . .

As a parent/autocratic boss, you are one up on your corporate counterparts. You don't need a retreat to experience experiential learning. You've likely taken your kid to indoor playgrounds, and mini-golf, on vacations . . . you may have even witnessed some picnic-table falling (okay, that was pushing, not falling, but it's the same basic idea). I've seen my teen son convince his younger brother to bounce up and down on an inflatable inner tube and then pull it away to watch him land on the sand on his butt, hard. Any lesson he can use in real life? Trust no one. Awesome.

Are there actually things that a family can learn on an off-site? Things they can take back home and into the rest of their lives? You've got time, right?

The Indoor Playground

It's normally covered in germs (that you can't see) and bodily fluids (that you can see, and smell). Sometimes it just has a certain *je ne sais quoi* (smell only). The kids will fight to get to the top of the slide first, the batteries on the two-rider cars will run out in the first half-hour, and the mandatory socks you're wearing don't match and have a gaping hole in the big toe. Never fear, you can buy another pair for only seven bucks if you have to. Someone else's kid is punching your kid, your daughter is having the biggest meltdown of her life in front of that perfect woman and her stupid perfect child, and you got nabbed by the Peanut Police on the way in for an errant granola bar lurking in the bottom of your purse.

Lesson learned: Life is messy and competitive, sometimes stinks, and always costs more than you think. The taking off of the shoes is symbolic for walking a mile in someone else's. Like that three-year-old who just toddled off in your Louboutins.

Mini-Golf

You take turns trying to hit a fluorescent golf ball into a hole with a bent metal stick. The hole is often only reached through a clown's mouth, a pirate ship, or a misplaced lighthouse.

Lesson learned: Getting the ball in the hole is never a sure thing. There's always some clown standing in the way of your success. Laughing at you. (Note to self: Share this one with teenagers first.)

Grocery Shopping

In my book *Shut Up and Eat!*, I dedicate an entire chapter to grocery shopping with children. It is called "Gateway to Hell." Taking your kids to the store with you is like a purchasing agent taking a summer intern on a buying trip to China. Their eyes bug out. They get over-stimulated, and you end up buying things you just don't need that are probably a little toxic.

Lesson learned: Life is full of options, colors, flavors, and noise. Try to focus, get in, get out, and take no prisoners. Or Gummy Bears.

Camping

The camping off-site should mostly be avoided. The family dynamics don't change, and, in addition, you're in a tiny tent, in a huge forest, washing dishes in a lake, going to the bathroom over a fallen tree log, and cursing yourself for not packing that (extra) box of chardonnay. Any minor issues you have with another member of the family will emerge – full-blown and with teeth – during a camping trip. Perhaps the purpose of these trips is to make us remember why we work so hard to have a non-leaking roof over our heads, a soft bed, warm blankets, and running water. Not to mention privacy, cleanliness, and nearby restaurants.

Lesson learned: Let's just call this the "Appreciation Off-Site" and move on.

Swimming Lessons

All children should learn how to swim. As an extension, all parents should have to go through the drama and trauma that swimming lessons can bring. From the first lessons (where you have to don your own swimsuit and get in the water with them and assorted pasty-white or hairy-backed parents) to dragging them through the suspicious warm water on the locker room floor to the 320-degree public viewing area, it's painful. It's also worth it.

Lesson learned: Sometimes you have to feel cold and wet to appreciate feeling warm and dry. Also, don't get caught without a razor.

Competitive Hockey

You have to get up earlier than you went to bed the night before, drive through snow and ice, and then sit in a cold arena and listen to other parents talk about the drills they put their kid through last week so that they won't embarrass themselves this week. The conversation is lame, the coffee is bad, and it's cold. Luckily, hockey only lasts for ten months a year.

Lesson learned: Don't sign your kid up for competitive hockey.

Vacation

So we take our kids and stuff them into an already over-loaded car and then yell, "Road trip!" There you are: beaming, maps and two-gallon coffee cups in hand. It can be fun to force *that* daughter to sit next to *that* son. Keep an eye out for kids who are turning a little green as they play just a bit too long with their electronic hand-held games. Are you there yet, are you there yet? No.

Lesson learned: Life is a highway. Enjoy the ride. Wear earplugs. Or at least get the good seat, farthest away from the gassy kid.

I need to expand on this last one just a bit, since vacations are, of course, the biggest of Corporate Family outings. Now, *vacation* is a term best used loosely when you're basically taking your "work" (children) on the road (or in a plane, on a ship, etc.) with you. Forget about the adage "what happens in Vegas stays in Vegas." When it comes to family vacations, you don't want to leave anything behind – not a child, not a bathing suit, not a toothbrush, and certainly not your established rules and routines. Is it a drag sticking to routines while on holidays? Absolutely. Is it worth it? One hundred percent. Sure, go a little crazy with food (and wine, for Mom and Dad only), but try to keep the lid on such things as:

- Letting the kids stay up hours later than they usually do. Any child under the age of three will not sleep in to make up for lost time, and they will be cranky. This is what that will look like:

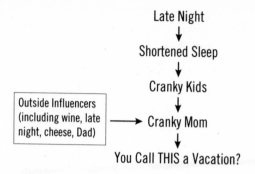

It's also important to keep some basic rules around meal time alive during a holiday. If soda pop is not allowed at breakfast at home, it's probably good to stick with that during a road trip as well. Finding the time to have at least one nutritious meal a day can make a big difference, both in your waistlines and in helping the kids feel good.

Personal hygiene is another thing you don't want to let go, particularly if you are dealing with teenage boys who have already minimized their shower- and tooth-brushing time to infinitesimal levels. If Wednesday is "shower night" at home, keep it going while you're away. Trick them into thinking a Tuesday is a Wednesday if the logistics don't work. What? You're the boss!

Is there a "lesson learned" for this entire section? As a matter of fact, there is. Most things we experience in life can offer up a lesson or two, if we're paying attention – and parents, by their very nature, experience more than most. You, Mom, live experiential learning. Embrace it, and don't be afraid to draw on and share your experience and expertise. Your junior employees will *love* that.

The Corporate Party

The cliché of the corporate holiday party is not as much of a cliché as you might think. It's totally built on facts: if you combine alcohol with pent-up human emotion and feelings (be they good or bad), you're going to get some drama. Fortunately, in the Corporate Family holiday party there are no romantic feelings to deal with, and the alcohol consumption is normally easily kept to just Mom and Dad. Mostly Mom. And maybe that one crazy uncle.

When you think about it, there's really no need for a Corporate Family Christmas Party. You're already giving them Christmas. Isn't that enough? Plus, we know who will be responsible for planning and cleaning up after this party. What, you have a family janitor? That's not you?

That being said, there's no reason we can't take some of the successful features of the corporate party and build them into the out-of-control world of kids' *birthday* parties (otherwise known as "the bane of your existence"). When I was a kid, girls had to wear a party dress and boys a little suit. We went to someone's house, played party games, ate cake, drank orange pop, opened presents, and went home. Today, the party is probably going to be at an "off-site" venue – indoor playground, laser parlor, hotel – and at least half of the kids will be wearing sweatpants. Sometimes this is the result of the party taking place at a gym facility, but mostly it's because forcing them to dress up would be wrong, somehow. The games are organized and supervised by trained staff, and pizza is always served. There will be a themed, store-bought, customized cake, which no child will eat, and they will grab their gigantic loot bags and head out the door before the birthday child has opened his or her presents. I'm not sure why parents don't want their kids to open the presents during the party; it's the perfect chance to say thanks to the giver and can easily kill twenty minutes, depending on the number of gifts.

So what aspects of a corporate party can we incorporate into the planning of a successful child's party?

- Dress code. While I'd steer clear of "black tie" or even "business formal," I would make them dress up a bit. Just do it. Comb their hair. At least change that stained T-shirt. Yours too, while you're at it.
- Have a seating plan for meals. Being on the social committee at work means you never have to sit next to the bore from IT at the holiday party. Being the mom/boss means that your child never has to sit next to that one kid who's a big rat or that girl whose nose is always running.
- Send invitations out far in advance. This is a no-brainer. We all have lives. We need to plan.
- Send RSVP reminders. People are just as clueless about real-life commitments as they are about work commitments. If you don't bug them, you'll end up with forty kids and only sixteen slices of pizza. You do not want this to happen. Ever.

- Keep your numbers in check (see above). No need to offer a "plus-one" option here. Who's the plus-one going to be? A sibling? A cousin? Someone's next-door neighbor? You don't need to deal with this. Keep to a firm "one guest per invite" policy.

- Start and end on time. If the party starts at 2:00 p.m., it starts at 2:00 p.m.. Don't punish the on-time kids by having them wait around to use the gym equipment or watch the clown because some clown of a parent is running late. End on time. Even if this means calling the parents and saying, "Your child is waiting outside the front door."

- Have a plan. You really don't want to wing it with a bunch of seven-year-old boys. Make a spreadsheet if you have to and pin it to the wall. These guys have the attention span of tsetse flies, so you want to make sure you're changing things up every fifteen minutes or so, or risk having material and collateral damage done to your home/the venue and/or an unsuspecting sibling.

- Have a budget and stick to it. Back on the finances. Who really wants the themed birthday decorations? You or the guest of honor? Make sure you're throwing a party for your child, not for the parents of the children who attend. Don't be afraid to put your foot down in terms of appropriate party expenses. What's wrong with an old-fashioned egg and spoon race? They can even use the spoons to eat the eggs afterwards.

- Consider issuing "drink tickets" but for soda or chips. No child needs more than one sugar-filled soda during a two-hour birthday party. Having them cash in tickets makes sure everyone gets their fare share.

Here's another idea! Why not think of your child's party as a promotion celebration? They're a year older, and hopefully a year wiser. As with every promotion, consider handing them a list of the new responsibilities they are expected to take on. A review of their job description might certainly be in order. Cheers!

The Company Picnic (Just Don't Do It)

This is a warning to all moms out there who might be thinking that a Corporate Family picnic is just what the doctor ordered. It's not. I'm serious. Here's why:

1) If warring children are tied together for the three-legged race, there will be no race. Just punching.

2) If you have trophies/ribbons for contests, someone is going to cry and someone is going to gloat, and, really, do your kids need more trophies? Don't they already have 127 lined up in their bedroom just for showing up?

3) Kids generally don't like potato salad. And potato salad is a mandatory food item at any company picnic. Problem.

4) There's really no reason to "dress cute" for a family company picnic now, is there? Mom? You too? Who are you trying to impress?

5) It's hard to catch a ride with someone who won't be drinking if there's only one other adult there. You will

both be drinking, just to get through the trophy throwing and the crying. And punching.

6) If it rains, it will be your fault. And you will suck.

7) Your kids will tell you that the food stinks, and you will tell them to shut up and eat.

8) Don't you have to eat most of your meals with these annoying people already? You need another one with them?

That's all. Enough said. You have been warned.

HOLD A FAMILY MEETING

The company outing or party is all about making life better for your employees (and, in turn, for you: happy employee equals happy boss). Sometimes, though, it's okay to amuse yourself – at their expense. Like making them climb through a rope spider web without touching it or play that game where they have to guess the name of the celebrity printed on the piece of paper taped to their back (Carrot Top for that guy!). A classic example on the home front is the Family Meeting.

Much has been said about this staple of Democratic Parenting. Democratic Parents see this as a forum for all voices to be heard and for all opinions to be shared. I have a couple of fundamental problems with this. I just don't think it's appropriate, or even a remotely good idea, to allow a six-year-old to have an equal voice with a thirty-six- or forty-six-year-old. Of course there's nothing wrong with listening to your children to see if there is a nugget of information or advice that can be shared, but the formality of the Family Meeting gives everyone the illusion of equal status at the table. I'd much rather solicit an opinion from my children when I need it – during a drive to hockey, while tucking them into bed, or even at the family mealtime – but in a much more casual way.

I believe the words *family* and *meeting* are contradictory. Bear with me. Here's a definition of a successful "meeting" from an old business textbook: "All important meetings have two requirements in common – an agenda for the orderly presentation of the topics to be discussed, and a chairman to monitor the discussions and give everyone a fair chance to speak."

I could write an entire book about the effectiveness (or lack thereof) of meetings in a corporate setting, and include a fair-sized appendix on the word *agenda* and its two separate but equally intriguing definitions (think *hidden* and you'll catch my drift, as well as an important parenting technique). But I'll save that for another time. Back to the Family Meeting. We all know what the word *family* means, so let's turn our attention to *meeting* instead: Do the words *orderly presentation* have anything to do with the discussions that happen around your dinner table during a family meeting? Does everyone get a fair chance to speak? Do kids *ever* think anything is fair? Should they even have a fair chance to speak?

Even in the most structured corporate meetings, many people spend their supposed "listening time" figuring out ways to "reload" their argument. But at least this is done mostly in a civilized and respectful manner (with the exception of the executive vice president I worked for at a large Canadian bank, who said to me and a colleague, "Why don't you tell me what your strategy was here, and then I'll tell you the correct one").

This may come as a huge surprise to some of you, but siblings don't generally feel that their counterparts have a valid opinion on anything. Attempting to get respect for conflicting opinions in this type of open forum often just ends with slapping and food throwing. Seeking out individual opinions, and then having the boss (that's you) weigh them and then share a *decision* (not a *suggestion*) with the family on where to go on vacation, or how to spend some additional money, is a task that belongs to you. You are the boss, remember? Say it with me.

But even I can wedge open my mind wide enough to admit that there are a *few* occasions in which a family meeting might be warranted. These include, but are not necessarily limited to:

- The discovery that a personal item owned by Mom has been lost, damaged, or altered in some way as to make it unusable. A review of the "what belongs to Mom, belongs to Mom" rule must be undertaken.
- It has been noted that each time the word *antique* is used, the children alternate between fits of giggles and

looks of horror. An investigation into the source of this reaction must be launched.

- None of the children complained about the dinner. An analysis of whether they are sick, guilty, or alien clones must be made.

Should any of these – or other viable scenarios – occur in your house, and the need for a family meeting is truly felt, here are my rules for getting it right. Feel free to post them on the fridge for all to see:

- Rule #1: The "Chairman" is me. Suck it up. Oh, and there's no Talking Stick (see Rule #5).
- Rule #2: I will have a Family Meeting only if I actually want your input. This is rare. If I have made a unilateral decision, you might get a memo in your mail slot. Or it might just hit you from out of the blue.
- Rule #3: "Input" is not "He's an idiot." That is an "insult." I can get that from you anytime; I don't need to call a Family Meeting. You know whom I'm talking to.
- Rule #4: The Family Meeting is mostly a one-way communication tool: my way to your way. No need to get back to me on anything. I'm good.
- Rule #5: If I have to introduce a Talking Stick, it won't be pretty.

Got that? Excellent. Have fun!

UNLEASH SOME BEST PRACTICES

Many companies engage in what they call "best practices." What this means is that processes that work successfully in one area of the business are duly (and sometimes done-to-death-ly) recorded and put into a report so that other areas of the business can learn, and ostensibly not make the same mistakes as their flummoxed predecessors. Best practices are often shared between companies as well, and even across industries.[97] Think of the production line that Henry Ford pioneered with his Model T car – it's probably the most famous example of a best practice in action.

All baby and parenting books are basically best-practices manuals in disguise. And, frankly, they're just about as effective as a bank taking a best-practices guide from a retail store and expecting to apply the same principles to their own, radically different, business. Babies and children are unique, which means that when it comes to raising the little darlings, we need to be the authors of our own best practices. A spot of bad news here: the best-practices guide for Child #1 will not work on Child #2. At all. You need a different guide for each one. Have I mentioned that babies were born to destroy every parenting theory – or best practice – ever invented?

All of this being said, I'd still fully support a more general *Best Practices for Families* document that would provide me

....

[97] This has always perplexed me.

and many other desperate parents with much-needed short-
cuts and advice in several critical areas:

- How much is too much? We all want our kids to have fun,
  and to develop a good sense of humor. Telling Mom her
  butt is bigger than the wide screen TV? Hi-lar-i-ous.
  Telling Dad the glare off his forehead is causing early
  blindness? Hys-ter-i-cal. Reminding Mom that she's old
  enough to be the teacher's mother, but she still has to call
  them Mr. or Ms.? Too funny. But joking about Mom not
  having anything "better to do" than drive you to the mall?
  So not funny. Tell your children that if they ever "go
  there," they will most definitely not be "going" to the mall.
  Best Practice: Children should never, ever, suggest that
  their parents aren't busy, or that they don't work hard.
  They do. Also, no one should tease a teenage girl. Ever.[98]
- Dress code. Ah, the slippery slope. You want your kids
  to look cool, right? You just don't want your daughter to
  look like a skank or your son to look like a gang member.
  The tricky part here is defining what cool is – for you
  and for your child. Surprisingly, they have different
  ideas on this than we do. Finding common ground
  can be hard.
  Best Practice: I started giving my kids a clothing allowance
  when they turned thirteen – old enough to shop the mall
  and buy what they want, without dragging me around. If

....

[98] Trust me.

they wanted to spend the whole thing on a pair of runners and forgo the much-needed package of new underwear, it was their call. They became their own Budget Controllers. In the corporate world, this is called "empowerment."[99]

- Nerdy versus cool. I know, I know. It seems appealing to have your sixteen-year-old at home with you on a Saturday night playing Scrabble, but if you allow or, worse, encourage this, chances are good that you'll have a forty-year-old at home with you, playing digital Scrabble in the basement. For a living. Surrounded by his *Star Wars* action figures.

  Best Practice: Encourage them to have a social life, and to find kids to hang out with. Here's the thing: Once they're past the age of ten, you don't get to choose who they like or don't like. Or, in fact, who or what they find cool. The more you try to define "cool" from a parental perspective, the further away the object, pastime, or person will become. Note: Other kids' parents are *always* cooler than you. Not sure why. Mostly because they're not you. Don't spend time worrying about it or trying to fix it. I guarantee you one of *your* kids' friends think you're cooler than *her* mom. It evens out.

- It's all relative. No one drives you crazier than your own mother, right? One day I discovered, to my amazement, that just by standing in the kitchen, by merely

....

[99] Don't "empower" your kids too much. That becomes Democratic Parenting.

existing, I was driving my teen son nuts. I'll admit that part of me was kind of thrilled, and part was kind of disappointed. Then I realized it was a Best Practice being handed to me on a silver platter!

Best Practice: *Know* the disdain! Embrace it! And employ it when it works to your advantage.

- Male prioritization. Men have an uncanny ability to pinpoint the ideal time for cleaning out the back corner of the garage. No, no, it's not when you need the storage space in the winter . . . it's twenty minutes before you have fourteen people coming over for dinner – probably from his side of the family (a situation that may well have instigated this natural flight to an outdoor space). Finding a Best Practice that would allow men to get work done around the house at the right time and in the *right order* would be infinitely helpful to most women I know. Perhaps we should strike a committee.

Why not develop your own Best-Practice Guide? Learn what each junior employee is best at and have that employee train the others. Mastery of tasks such as making beds, clearing tables, and vacuuming are encouraged; farting on demand and eating things in just one bite are not. If your child knows she's the "best" at something, she will do her best to retain her Jedi-like status and keep up the standard. Just try it.

WRITE A ONE-PAGER

A what? In the business world, a "one-pager" is a directive of sorts – a summary of all relevant information on a particular topic or procedure. Once a one-pager has been issued, there is no room for argument. Autocracy at its best. Let's consider a one-pager for a typical "around the house" situation.

Situation: Clarifying why children need to bathe on a regular basis, and why everyone in the household is entitled to inform those children who stink that they need to do it. Including the father of these children, who also needs to know when the last bath or shower took place. We know, so he should too. Write it down if you have to. Apparently the sniff test is not working.

One-Pager: Bathing Schedule

1) Babies need to be bathed daily only if they happen to be your firstborn. Frankly, it gives you something to do with them. Spoiler alert: If you're pregnant with your first, you should know that newborns are really boring. Also extremely challenging. You'll see what I mean.

2) After the firstborn, and with older children, bathing needs to take place on a semi-regular basis. A child needs bathing every few days even if he or she doesn't stink. There could be dirt anywhere. *Anywhere*. Literally, *anywhere*. Surprising, I know. Timing is flexible but is generally based on dirt accumulation, where the child is on the toilet-training spectrum, and his or her level of

personal care. The time frame shortens considerably and somewhat alarmingly with the onset of puberty.

3) A note for Dad: Saying, "Well, you didn't tell me he needed to take a bath/shower" when your wife returns from a night out is not a valid excuse. It's an insult. To yourself, as well as to her. (And they wonder why we nag.)

4) If your normally blond child's hair looks Goth, it needs a wash. It's not Goth; it's grease.

5) If you ask a school-age child when her last bath or shower was and she pauses for even three seconds before answering, it's been too long. Start running the water.

6) Swimming is great. Swimming, however, is *not* a bath or shower unless there is actual soap and shampoo involved. Use a garden hose for rinsing if you have to. I'm good with that.

7) Yes, you have to do this all over again in a couple of days.

In the interests of time and space, and because I think you get the point, I will resist the urge to do more of these. Although you know the one on "Peeing Into, and Not Around, the Toilet" would have been good, right?

DEVISE A GUIDE TO CORPORATE LINGO

This is just pure fun, plain and simple. One of the secret beauties of working in an office is deciphering the lexicon. It's unique, it's hilarious, and it's remarkably descriptive.

Please note that this effort is not to be shared with junior employees or middle managers. This is strictly for the bi-weekly inter-industry "executive" meeting that takes place at the coffee shop/bar/mani-pedi place. Can't be giving away your secrets to just anyone!

Useful Acronyms

- **KISS Principle**: You're thinking, "Keep It Simple, Stupid," but we're not supposed to use the word *stupid* in relation to our children . . . something about self-esteem. So, this is actually just the kiss principle. When kids are hurt, you kiss them where it hurts (using some discretion depending on cleanliness and location of body part). When they're sad, you tell them things to make them happy or you give them money. Works surprisingly well.
- **BISS Principle**: "Because I Said So." Can only be used by Mom. Why? BISS. Catching on yet? I would love for it to actually stand for "Because It's Stupid, Simpleton," but this isn't allowed (see KISS).
- **DAD**: "Dad's at Depot," as in Home Depot. As in, where else would he be when you need to get something done on a weekend? Blame it on DAD.
- **WINE**: "Wine Is Necessary Every Day." Don't argue with me on this one. It's not worth it. BISS.
- **PIP**: "Parenting in Public." You know, where we pretend to be nice parents and whisper our threats instead of screaming them. Use of the word *darling* is

recommended, and an overemphasis on *please* and *thank you* is mandatory.

- **PIPX**: "Parenting in Private." The X covers some Extreme Parenting methods that might take place only behind closed doors and shut windows.

- **WWKD**: "What Would Kathy Do?" Want to know how to figure this one out? It's alarmingly simple: Look for a) the easiest thing to do and b) the thing that benefits you the most. For example, I love my hairdresser because she gives me wine. Even when my kids are getting their cuts done, and I'm just sitting there. Because of this, you'll never find me at a kid-centric hair salon with merry-go-round ponies and racing-car chairs. They don't serve wine. Crazy, right? Please feel free to substitute your own first initial here when making crucial decisions, particularly on behalf of your husband.

- **WWMHD**: "What Would My Husband Do?" While this question could yield entirely unsatisfying results when considering things like whether you need another pair of black shoes, it can come in handy when trying to sort out what to do when something has spilled (just leave it, it'll dry anyway), when kids are engaged in perilous activities (they're kids, they'll be fine, what's the worst . . . oops), or what to make for dinner (pass the phone). This filter can provide an unexpected level of relief. Try it. Right now.

- **WTF**: Really? You had to read the explanation for this one? What kind of crazy perfect parenting world do you live in?

Useful Jargon

- **"It's all about the optics."** In the business world, this means: Yes, this whole project could be a complete screw up, but as long as it *looks* good, let's go for it. Alternately, it can mean it's the most well-executed project *ever*, and will be revolutionary in scope, but if it makes me/us look bad in any way, we're going to scrap it. At home, bad optics include: getting caught wearing fleece and Crocs; your child telling a neighbor she ate Beefaroni for breakfast; getting caught saying, "Gee, since I can't pull a piece of bristol board out of my ass, I guess you're out of luck" (yes, optics can be audio too); or getting caught texting through your kid's solo performance during the "Holiday Night of Magic" concert. The key words here? *Getting caught.*

- **"I'm not married to it."** At work, this is used to distance yourself from a project or strategy that you had previously supported. You're now backpedalling as you've come to realize that it's, well, horrible. At home, announcing that you're not "too married" to "it" might be a bad thing to say to your spouse. And it would be downright creepy if you said it about one of your kids. Or a dog. Perhaps this one should stay in the boardroom.

- **"Reading from the same page," "Singing from the same songbook."** These terms are used to indicate that no matter what kind of corporate garbage you might be spewing, you are taking the guy on the other end of the phone, or across from you at the boardroom table, down *with* you. It's like a pinky-swear where you both agree to agree. I like to use this one at home for more practical purposes – for example, when I'm lying in bed reading with my son and simultaneously going through my Twitter feed or checking my BlackBerry. He looks up and says, "You're not even listening, Mom," and I say, "Of course I am. I'm on the same page. I see that pigeon and the bus. What a rascal." This works especially well if you've read the same book about eight thousand times. Which most of us have. There is an upside.[100]

- **"Partners in crime."** Corporately, this is usually said, tongue-in-cheek, about two or more people who seem to be inexplicably linked on some project or strategy. There is something covert about it, and probably not really appropriate. At home, this term could be used for those two rotten kids who just shot toothpaste all over the bathroom. Guess what? Now they're "partners in punishment."

- **"Strategic thinking."** Anyone who has to define the way in which they are thinking likely doesn't have much capacity in the thinking department. Isn't all thinking strategic? If I slide to the left when I'm changing this baby-boy's diaper, I won't get pee in my eye. If I turn the clocks back half an hour I can have the kids in bed in time to watch *The Good Wife*. If I tell my husband I sent

....

[100] It can be hard to know if you're in fact "Singing from the same songbook" when dealing with a child or an atonal parent. Try it anyway.

him an e-mail two weeks ago about going out tonight, he'll believe me for fear of being called inattentive again. It all works. For once I'd love to hear someone say, "I wasn't thinking about that strategically at all. I was just hungry/wanted a promotion."

Had enough yet? I know I have, but there's a reason business people use these expressions. They cloak the real meaning of what they're saying so they can easily weasel out of working on a project by stating you must have misunderstood them at the last meeting. Now this is an idea I can get behind – and it could work beautifully in the parenting world as well. For example:

- **"That's a Dad project."** Actually, I can probably build that solar-powered car model faster and more efficiently than your dad, but I just can't be bothered, and it gives him the chance to bond (i.e., "babysit") with you while I troll Twitter or open a bottle of wine.
- **"I'll be with you in a minute, honey."** If I'm doing something unpleasant, like filling out camp forms, it really will be just a minute. If I'm in the middle of a good e-mail exchange with a friend, or watching to see what that nasty Real Housewife is about to do, a *minute* is a relative term and could last up to sixty of them. And beyond.
- **"We'll see."** Okay, honestly, this means no, but I just can't be bothered to deal with your reaction/tantrum right now. I might turn this into a "Dad project."

- **"Are you in their family?"** Used when the kids point out something that another family does that they think is superior to the way in which you run your own family. This could be something small, such as serving chocolate milk at dinner, or something big, such as letting the children choose the destination of the next family vacation. What it really means is, "Okay, we think those people are idiots, and there's no way in hell that's going to happen around here."
- **"You must be proud of yourself."** This one can go two ways, depending on tone. Sometimes we really mean it (hey, a good mark, for once), and sometimes it's derogatory (you made your brother cry, again). I suggest letting the kids figure out which way we're going. They learn.
- **"He needs to feel better about himself."** This comes in handy when your child tells you about his braggart friend who is constantly talking about his own accomplishments and putting others down. What we're thinking is, "and we know where he gets that from, don't we? His mother is a piece of work."

The only thing that works better both in the work world and at the home front than anger is ambiguity. Take on as many of these as you can and confuse your employees into thinking they've done the right thing, but that you're still the boss.

GET OUT OF DODGE

Okay, I've saved the very best of the already very best section for last. When your junior employees are falling down on the job, when your middle manager needs to be demoted due to gross incompetence, when things just suck so bad you can't stand them anymore, take advantage of the one perk that every boss holds in his or her back pocket – the business trip.

Not long ago, I was sitting in an airport lounge, eating salted almonds and sipping a glass of chardonnay. A slight delay in my departure gave me ample opportunity to reflect on the many times I've heard husbands and corporate types complain about the rigors of business travel. Now, don't get me wrong – I know there's nothing glamorous about staying in a sterile hotel near the airport in Winnipeg,[101] but the fact of the matter is, you're away from home and released from the day-to-day responsibilities of running the house, chauffeuring the kids, overseeing the homework, etc. Oh wait, I went and presupposed that dads are usually engaged in these types of activities on a regular basis. Are they? Here's the thing: If business travel doesn't feel like a break to you, you're not pulling your fair share at home, no matter who you are, or where you're traveling to. Most moms would take that hotel room on the strip in The Peg (or, dare

....

[101] I grew up in Winnipeg. Save your cards and letters. I know.

I say, Saskatoon[102]) over having to manage the practicalities of the home front. In fact, I'd go so far as to say that business travel for most moms is sort of like summer camp. Let me explain. I might be writing this on the back of a napkin in the Hotel 88 in Moose Jaw, but it's still valid – see how much I can get done without the kids running around or the washing machine timer going off?

Six Reasons Why Business Trips Are Like Summer Camp for Moms

1) While away on a business trip, you have a set schedule of activities to accomplish during the day. At camp, these activities are listed on a sheet hung by the cabin door, and there is little flexibility. On a business trip, these activities have been entered into your smartphone, and there is a tight schedule. This is a good thing. At home, flexibility comes in the form of flying milk containers, random bodily function expulsions, and unforeseen trips to the skate-sharpening place. And all of these happen in direct proportion to the amount of work you need to get done at a particular time. Who needs flexibility? Here at Business Travel Summer Camp, your time is your own. Your biggest challenge might be that the mini-bottle of wine in the bar fridge is a sauvignon blanc, and you really were in a pinot grigio type of mood. *Ahhhhh!*

....

[102] I did not grow up there. Go ahead.

2) Someone else prepares your meals. Oh, this is huge. And, yes, while the Chef's Special at the SleepEez Motel on Route 814 in northern Alberta might have as its base ingredient the same Hamburger Helper you have in your cupboard at home, you don't care. You didn't have to make it. You also can't read the calorie count on the packaging it came in, and you don't have to clean it up afterwards. Did I mention you probably have a glass of wine in your hand and nowhere to drive to? Where's the downside? The worst meals served to you outside of the house are better than the best meals you have to make at home yourself. If "yourself" is me, that is. At a real summer camp, your meals are prepared en masse, and there's little choice offered, if any. But even your pickiest of eaters will tell you that the food served at summer camp is awesome. Why? Because they are hungry and they didn't have Mom running around fetching them snacks in between lunch and dinner, during the soccer game, and while taking a three-minute walk to the neighborhood park. The enjoyment of food is not entirely flavor based; it's circumstance based as well.

3) Campers are often told that they must be responsible for their actions, and that they alone can control their reactions to how others treat them. Cabinmates often have to agree to disagree and get along for the sake of cabin harmony. This should be the case during business travel as well. We need to control our reactions when we get bumped off a flight, put in the room next

to the elevator, or are forced to deal with a dirty fork. First of all, you're not traveling with children so all of this is trivial, and secondly, it still beats being at home, where you are constantly being held responsible for things that are not your fault, such as:

a) Moving dirty sweatshirts from the front hall to the laundry basket where they might unfortunately get cleaned.

b) Stealing someone's Hot Wheels track. We know what you do with your spare time, Mom.

c) Throwing out an art installation that included toilet rolls, massive amounts of Scotch tape, and a tampon box.

d) Everything that went wrong with the twelve-year-old's math test.

See? It's all good! Make friends with your fellow stranded travelers and find peace and harmony over a fine merlot.

4) There's usually at least one kumbayah moment with another person at camp, someone who becomes your instant Summertime Best Friend. This phenomenon also occurs on business trips that include groups. This bonding could take place in a bar, although for safety and pride reasons it is recommended that when occurring between members of the opposite sex, such a moment should take place within a business setting or at a minimum over tea in the hotel lobby, not in the Hooters down the street. Ah, the Business-Trip Best

Friend: you'll share confidences, laughs, and personal confessions. Then you'll get on separate planes and not exchange more than a "How's it going?" the next time you see them. Except for that one lame inside joke that will carry on well past its shelf-life because neither one of you knows how to let it go.

5) If you get a little dirty at camp, no one cares. In a physical sense, at any rate. On a business trip, you can get a little dirty, or rather salty, with your language, since your kids are not around. You could say the F-word. In a meeting. Without having to deposit money into the swearing box, apologize to the kids, or suffer being snickered at by the teenagers. In fact, swearing *about* your children while you're *away* from your children is almost encouraged. You can take off your "Mommy Guard" and let loose. At least a little. Damn it. Gosh darn.

6) You go to bed exhausted and you wake up way too early. Campers love to stay up whispering to each other (about who sucked at field hockey, that sort of thing), just like moms jump at the chance to hang out with adults, whose food they don't have to cut up, and who don't argue with you about why you can have another glass of wine, but they can't have another pop. This can lead to a "But I'm in Detroit" mentality, which in turn can result in mini-bar raids and all-night movies, not to mention the ill-advised "Let's go clubbing with the guys from accounting" outings. But remember: what happens at camp, stays at camp. Unfortunately, what happens on business trips

gets rehashed and embellished during the next business trip, over drinks with your next new Business-Trip Best Friend. Be careful.

See? Why wouldn't any boss/mom want to get away? I'd suggest booking a trip even if things are hunky-dory at home. Oh . . . and make sure your destination is somewhere you need to fly to. *But planes are terrible*, you're saying. I will concede that air travel today is not glamorous. At all. The terminals are crowded, the lines are long, the employees are surly, the food is crappy, and the drinks are not free. However, once you have experienced air travel under warlike conditions (i.e., traveling with young children), waiting to board a plane solo seems like a pleasant experience. No matter that your flight has been delayed for three and a half hours, that the coffee you bought tastes like tar, or that the man in the seat next to you smells like he just participated in GarlicFest. I can always tell who the moms are at the gate of a delayed plane. A small half-smile normally appears on their lips as they crack open a new paperback or return to their laptop or BlackBerry to let the home front know they'll be on their own for dinner. This might be the only "me time" many moms get. Being forced to have downtime, even in a crowded, dirty, public transportation hall, is not all bad. My recent discovery of a little retail service chain called "10 Minute Manicure" has made the experience all the more lovely.

And if we're sitting next to somebody else's tired and cranky child? All the better! It's positively wonderful to be able to pass out a sympathetic smile to the harried mom, or even talk to the little bastard for a few minutes; you don't have to be responsible for them on the plane, while waiting for bags, or getting through the customs lineup. You can be just that benevolent. Awesome.

If you don't work in a business that requires you to travel, find a reason to travel. And let's all start working on that camp song (what rhymes with *escape?*).

REAL-LIFE LESSON

When my third child, Bridget, was about six months old, I had to go on a business trip to Whistler, B.C. Of course, right in the middle of the evening festivities — I mean Learning Activity — I got a phone call from my husband saying he could not get her to settle for the night. Being all bosslike, I told him to be strong and let her cry it out. He did. And the next morning, he went into her room to find her covered in dried vomit. This was apparently my fault. So it's never a bad idea for Mom to go on a business trip. Even if everything that goes wrong at home is her fault, she isn't the one cleaning it up.

CONCLUSION

Congratulations! You've made it through my manifesto (or "mommyfesto," perhaps). Hopefully, you've already started to see yourself as the boss. If you haven't figured this out yet, here's a hint: a big part of *being* the boss is *feeling* like the boss. And if you don't feel like it quite yet, don't worry too much. Do what most newly minted supervisors and managers do and fake it till you make it. If you're not leading, no one is going to follow.

So how can you tell if you're on the road to success? Look for these eight simple signs:

1) You believe that there should be a boss in your family (and that You. Are. It.).

- You've come to understand that "Because I said so" is a valid response to just about any question, and that it does not, ever, require a debate. Open discussions are fine but only on issues that are actually open for discussion. You do not engage in arguments/conversations that have only one outcome – the one that you chose. You can, of course, inform your worthy opponent (that snarling four-year-old or smirking teen) that they can talk, and you will listen, but that on a particular matter (say, for instance, switching bedrooms with Mom and Dad), you will *never* change your mind.

- You know better than your kids on pretty much any subject.[103]
- You've accepted that the Autocratic Parenting model is not only logical but highly desirable.

2) You know what you want to achieve.
- You've set annual, weekly, or daily goals and established processes and systems to help you achieve them; you revisit these goals when a new demand on your time occurs. Some demands we can choose and some we can't. You know this and realize that you can't do *everything* you want to do.
- You've formally divided your domestic responsibility assignments. And you are now letting them (kids and Dad) own it (whatever "it" might be). If you don't like the way he's doing the laundry, you know you can either take it back entirely (and trade it for something else, like toilet cleaning) or suck it up and accept that this is the trade-off for not having to do it. You're learning that sucking it up is oftentimes worth it.

....

[103] With the possible exception of the appropriate use of the word *totes*. Maybe someone can explain that one to me.

- Your kids' extracurricular activities are manageable, both time- and cost-wise. Every new activity has been entered into with the knowledge that it may not continue the following year if a) there has been an extra and unacceptable time commitment, b) there have been extra and unacceptable costs incurred, c) the participating child has whined more than twice about doing the activity, d) there is no Wi-Fi at the facility, or e) the other parents are simply too annoying.[104]

- In the car, you are in charge of seating arrangements, temperature control, window openings, and media. You don't have to listen to more than one Justin Bieber song in a row. Unless you want to. Whatever. I'm not judging.[105]

- You've stopped taking on responsibilities that belong to others and have started focusing on what you, the boss, have to do.

- You've become the Queen of Spreadsheets.

3) You've established clear expectations. For everyone.
    - The kids know (begrudgingly is absolutely fine) that you're the boss, and that they have a role that is *not* being the boss.
    - Bedtime is a time that *you* set. You stop telling people, "I can't get them to bed before X p.m." You

---

[104] Most common reason for not wanting to continue.
[105] Much.

can get them to bed, and they *can* choose to sleep or be tired in the morning.

- The kids know what is expected of them in any and all situations.
- *You* know what is expected of the kids in any and all situations.

4) You've set boundaries.
- Everyone is aware of punishments and probations, and knows these things *actually could happen*. And by "everyone," I mean the kids.
- You are in charge of setting and relaxing the boundaries.
- If there is an extraneous child at your house, you've approved of it, and you know how to get a hold of the parent at any time to end the session. If the parent is late picking up their child on more than two occasions (even if it doesn't really inconvenience you in any way), you stop having them over, and *you tell the parent why*.

5) You know (and respect) your own limits.
- You know you can't do it all, and you're okay with that.
- You are not making four different meals for four different children every single night. They don't have to like your choice of dinner; they just have to eat it. And how do we respond if they complain? Say it with me, sisters, "Shut up and eat!"
- You don't find yourself sitting in school meetings

that a) you don't want to be in and b) aren't included in your annual goals. If you want to be involved at the school, you've made sure you have the time to do it before you commit, not after.

- You have time to get to the gym. If you don't, you need to re-evaluate one of the ways you're not the boss of your own time. The president of the United States has time. You have time. Make the time.
- Your social life gets equal if not superior bearing to theirs. Repeat after me: "I shall not cancel or postpone a previously scheduled date (with myself or with friends) at the sudden appearance of a child's birthday party, hockey game, request for movie, or even slight illness. *Unless I want to.*"
- You know how to say "no" to things that are not your priority.
- You know how to say "yes" to things you want to make your priority.

6) Accomplishments are recognized and encouraged.
   - You've said goodbye to the "I'm so busy, but I don't get anything done" syndrome.
   - You know that success breeds success, and you know how to find success, even on the home front.

7) You enjoy the perks.
   - You are a benevolent dictator when the occasion calls for it.

- You can be spontaneous without giving away your power.

8) You've become a mentor.
   - You understand that empowering your children to do something themselves is much more effective that doing it for them.
   - You've passed this book on to other bosses in need.

So, how did you do? Have you got this boss thing sorted out, or do you still have a bit of work to do? Either way, it's good! You're making progress. Even the most experienced professionals can wait for years before being promoted to the position of CEO. And not all of them turn out to be *good* CEOs. This book isn't about finding a CEO to model yourself after; it's about finding a parenting style that is successful for you, and that makes you feel successful.

Do I always treat my children like employees? Of course not – they're children, and human as well. Do I expect things to run as smoothly as possible and to make my kids accountable, responsible, and ultimately successful? I do.

I know, I know. You're all dying to know if I actually use the phrase "I am so the boss of you" with my children. Absolutely. All the time! But as any good boss knows, one of the hallmarks of success is being open to new ideas. In parenting, too, a willingness to challenge traditional thinking is essential. Most kids are not traditional thinkers – surprise, surprise! – and believe it or not, moms/bosses can learn from them. I frequently adapt to my kids' way of thinking and I try never to dismiss ideas out of hand – unless those ideas involve me doing their work!

Are you feeling ready to take the world on and boss some people around? If so, here's my final gift to you: a certificate you can hang in your office/kitchen/car to make sure everyone is aware of your credentials. Otherwise, you're just going to have to keep reminding them that you are the boss. And, trust me, you have better things to do with your time.

ACKNOWLEDGMENTS

This book has been brewing for a while. Through every job I had, and through every parenting experience that, within itself, was a job. I couldn't have written this book without some very good bosses, and some very bad ones, not to mention some questionable parenting experiences (both my own, and those of others I've heard about), plus more than a few very good examples I see around me every day.

I need to thank: my Old Girls' Club (we're not old . . . but we're not really girls either): Theresa Albert, Julie Cole, Alyson Schafer, Sharon Vinderine, Heather Greenwood-Davis, Jo-Anne Wallace, Racheal McCaig, Tracy Ruiz, and Maureen Dennis; my literary agent, Hilary McMahon, and my speaking and corporate agent, Heather MacLean, who continue to have faith in selling me, and finding elusive buyers for what I do, as well. And of course the editor who just can't quit me (I keep stalking her), Linda Pruessen.

I'm also lucky to have the support of a gaggle of terrific BFF's – Robyn "Wanna Be Bad Tonight" Campbell, Cathy "Is It Friday Yet" Buckland-Coles, Orysa "Polyvore Pro"

Steele, Jamie "Crazy Lady" Harada, Heather "UV Couture" McCartney, and Robbie "Pumpkin Dent" Saunders.

I believe in mentoring. Please keep a lookout for my pals and mentorees Kelli Catana, Adam Lanteigne, Leigh Mitchell, and Samantha Monpetit Hyunh. They're going places – go along with them.

Most of all, my own staff/family: my husband and co-boss (*hahahaha*, not really), Steve Webster; my beautiful and inspiring daughter, Victoria; my optimistic and outward-bound son, Alexander; my culinary hockey-playing daughter, Bridget; and my swashbuckling son, Nicholas. Thanks for the guidance and training from my original supervisors, my mum and dad, Jill and John Buckworth.

And of course to every mom or dad who said to their child, "Where would YOU like to go for dinner, sweetie?" I thank you for the inspiration.

Want to keep the conversation going? Use the hashtag #AmSoTheBoss every time you have a "Boss" moment with your own family, and make sure to cc @KathyBuckworth so I can read and share it too.

Kathy Buckworth is an award-winning writer, public speaker, spokesperson, and television personality. She is a columnist for Sympatico.ca, *Metro News*, *GoodLife Magazine*, and *ParentsCanada*. She also contributes to the *Huffington Post*, *Dabble Magazine*, and the *Toronto Star*. She is a featured parenting expert on *CityLine* and appears on CTV News Channel, *Canada AM*, and *Breakfast Television*. Kathy is the author of six books: *The Secret Life of Supermom*, *Supermom*, *Journey to the Darkside*, *The BlackBerry Diaries*, *Shut Up and Eat!*, and *I Am So the Boss of You*.

Kathy spent eighteen years in corporate marketing and applies these management skills with varying degrees of success on her four children.

Visit www.kathybuckworth.com and follow Kathy on Twitter @KathyBuckworth.